Distributed by
Motorbooks International
Publishers & Wholesalers Inc.
Osceola, Wisconsin 54020, USA

FIRST PRINTING
June 1975

SECOND PRINTING
May 1976

the real CORVETTE

other books by Ray Miller:

FROM HERE TO OBSCURITY
Model T

HENRY'S LADY
Model A

THE V-8 AFFAIR
Pre-war V-8's

THUNDERBIRD!
Ford's T-Bird

NIFTY FIFTIES FORDS
Post-war V-8's

the real CORVETTE

An Illustrated History of Chevrolet's Sports Car

By RAY MILLER

and additional photographs by GLENN EMBREE

THE EVERGREEN PRESS
Oceanside, California

the real CORVETTE

an illustrated history of Chevrolet's Sports Car

First Printing
June 1975

Library of Congress Catalog Card Number 75-8100
ISBN 0-913056-06-5

Printed by:
 Sierra Printers, Inc.
 Bakersfield, California

Printed in U.S.A.

The Evergreen Press
Oceanside, California

RAY MILLER, along with Bruce McCalley, another Founding Member of the Model T Ford Club of America, produced *FROM HERE TO OBSCURITY*, a book that has become the Standard Reference for those interested in the Model T Ford. From there, it was a relatively modest effort for him to turn his talents to coverage of the Model A in *HENRY'S LADY*, the pre-war V-8 cars in *The V-8 AFFAIR*, and later the post-war Fords with The *NIFTY FIFTIES* and *THUNDERBIRD!* in all of which he collaborated with Glenn Embree. Their work has been assembled as The Ford Road Series, the five volumes of which have been described as "the greatest collection of detailed information" on the Ford automobiles. With this book, the pair turn their attention to the products of General Motors.

Ray has been interested in cars for many years. In the past he has owned many Chevrolets as well as Fords, but of these, remembers best "tooling around all of one summer in a battered '56 'Vette". At present his collection, limited only by storage space, includes a 1910 Model T Ford, a '36 phaeton, '57 T-Bird, and his "modern" car, a 1954 Skyliner in which he pursues his daily efforts.

In addition to having had the responsibility for the text and production of this book, including many of the photographs, it was Ray who located the cars used to illustrate this work. His ability to find exactly the right cars, clearly demonstrated in the past, is enhanced by the fact that in Southern California there are so very many original, unrestored, and un-modified cars still being driven daily on the freeways. Likely a project of this sort could be undertaken only in this area.

GLENN EMBREE, well known professional photographer, counts among his clients many of the country's largest consumer goods manufacturers who often turn to him for photographic illustrations of their products to be used for advertising purposes. Fundamentally interested in Photographic Essays, his unusual perception generally provides uniquely interesting views.

Co-Author, with Ray Miller, of *THE V-8 AFFAIR, HENRY'S LADY, THUNDERBIRD!*, and *The NIFTY FIFTIES*, Glenn has established an enviable pattern of photographic reporting which is continued in this book. Although his Studio, in Hollywood, California, is adorned with portraits of well-known celebrities, it is apparent that Glenn *enjoys* his automotive portraiture as his pictures exhibit an interest and excitement that would otherwise be lacking.

Glenn has had a long-continuing relationship with Detroit. His special skills with illustrative photography were extensively used by Chevrolet (as well as Ford and Studebaker) in the promotion of the early Corvettes. The photograph on the cover of this book, as well as those on pages 10 & 11, were posed and photographed by Glenn in late *1957* in connection with the upcoming introduction of the 1958 Corvette.

The Author wishes to thank the many people who enthusiastically embraced the concept of this book from the start and whose encouragement and aid went so far towards making it a better book than it might have been. The Owners of the cars are generally mentioned in the text, but again we wish to thank them for their willingness to permit us to climb over, around, under, and behind their cars as we obtained the necessary illustrations. Their participation in this effort is sincerely appreciated by the writer. In addition we wish to thank:

The CHEVROLET MOTOR DIVISION whose originality in producing the Corvette led the way for the Industry, and whose publicity and public relations departments have been of so much recent assistance.

JOE PIKE, editor of CORVETTE NEWS, Chevrolet's prestigious and authoritative magazine who helped to confirm many of our findings and who furnished the corrected production figures which appear later in this book.

BILL WEYERS of Sales, and ERMA DENNIS of the Parts Department, of WESELOH CHEVROLET COMPANY in Oceanside, both of whom greatly aided us in comfirming characteristics and locating authentic models.

BOB WINGATE of Glendora, California, who early recognized the need for such a book as this and not only provided cars of his own for study, but sought out and recommended cars owned by others of his wide acquaintance.

LARRY CORNELL of San Bernardino whose extensive collection of automotive miniatures includes those used to illustrate the article found in this book.

JAY LAMKA of the NATIONAL COUNCIL OF CORVETTE CLUBS, JIM PRATHER of VETTE VUES, and ED THIEBAUD of the VINTAGE CORVETTE CLUB OF AMERICA all provided an enthusiastic response to our initial survey of interest in this book, and Ed provided helpful information relative to the earliest of 'Vettes.

DAN SMITH, Associate Editor of VETTE VUES, not only opened his sizeable inventory of new parts for detail study, and provided his car for a model, but also submitted pages of notes for cross-checking against our findings.

Professor DAVID L. LEWIS of the University of Michigan conducted on our behalf an interview with Zora Arkus-Duntov which resulted in our Chapter entitled "The Marque of Zora".

And finally,

ZORA ARKUS-DUNTOV, recently retired from Chevrolet, who will be remembered fondly by those who know the special thing that *is* Corvette.

IN preparing this material, the author has attempted to locate unrestored, low mileage original cars wherever possible. When failing in this he has employed as models restorations which are believed to be of the highest quality.

As is to be expected, there may well be items of incorrect data or style on a given automobile. Original cars may well have been modified to suit the convenience of an earlier owner; restorations are generally done to the best level of information available to the restorer, but occasionally a slip-up, sometimes of frightening proportions will occur.

We have *attempted* to screen the inaccuracies; we trust that we have succeeded in the effort. This book was intended to be what it is, a compendium of information which will enable an observer to identify, and to classify, both cars and parts. If there are errors, they are not to our knowledge.

The Chevrolet Corvette is more than just a fine automobile. It is a legend in its own time. My involvement with the Corvette included helping to form a Corvette Club (Corvette-Chattanooga). It was through association with that Club that I met my wife, Betty.

My first Corvette was a used '62. The '62 had always been *the* Corvette to me, partially because I was an avid TV watcher of "Route 66", and that was the model used on the show. From my first (and still very much remembered) '62, I've gone through five more Corvettes. Today, Betty and I enjoy our '63 Coupe.

The uniqueness of mass produced, glass-reinforced plastic bodied automobiles, combined with styling that lead the Industry, captured the hearts of thousands of soon-to-be Corvette Enthusiasts.

The Corvette has been called "The Real McCoy", "America's Only Sports Car", and "The American Dream," but no matter *what* you call it, the Corvette *is* an Automotive Classic. It is one of few automobiles ever produced that generates its own excitement and makes driving something more than just going from point A to point B.

Participate in the 23 years of Corvette excitement as you read and enjoy—
The Real CORVETTE

Chula Vista, California
June, 1975

Daniel D. Smith
Associate Editor
Vette Vues Magazine

9

It was early Fall of 1957, and the camera of Glenn Embree was employed to provide illustrations for a coming advertising campaign for the strikingly attractive new 1958 Corvette. The place, the legendary Mulholland Drive high above the San Fernando Valley where the tortuous twists and turns of the gravelled dirt road suggested an attractive scene.

Glenn's special abilities with the camera provided these two shots, recently extracted from a corner of his extensive files. The details of the photograph at the right clearly emphasizes the long, low, rakish character of the Corvette especially when compared to the Porsch at the rear left, but the true flavor of Corvette _driving_ is caught in only a glance at the photo below.

THE SECRET LIFE OF WALTER MITTY

"We're going through!" The Commander's voice was like thin ice breaking. He wore his full-dress uniform, with the heavily braided white cap pulled down rakishly over one cold gray eye. "We can't make it, sir. It's spoiling for a hurricane, if you ask me." "I'm not asking you, Lieutenant Berg," said the Commander. "Throw on the power light! Rev her up to 8,500! We're going through!" The pounding of the cylinders increased: ta-pocketa-pocketa-pocketa-*pocketa-pocketa*. The Commander stared at the ice forming on the pilot window. He walked over and twisted a row of complicated dials. "Switch on No. 8 auxiliary!" he shouted. "Switch on No. 8 auxiliary!" repeated Lieutenant Berg. "Full strength in No. 3 turret!" shouted the Commander. "Full strength in No. 3 turret!" The crew, bending to their various tasks in the huge, hurtling eight-engined Navy hydroplane, looked at each other and grinned. "The Old Man'll get us through," they said to one another. "The Old Man ain't afraid of Hell!" . . .

"Not so fast! You're driving too fast!" said Mrs. Mitty. "What are you driving so fast for?"

"Hmm?" said Walter Mitty. He looked at his wife, in the seat beside him, with shocked astonishment. She seemed grossly unfamiliar, like a strange women who had yelled at him in a crowd. "You were up to fifty-five," she said. "You know I don't like to go more than forty. You were up to fifty-five." Walter Mitty drove on toward Waterbury in silence, the roaring of the SN202 through the worst storm in twenty years of Navy flying fading in the remote, intimate airways of his mind. "You're tensed up again," said Mrs. Mitty. "It's one of your days. I wish you'd let Dr. Renshaw look you over."

With warm affection for his work, the Author happily dedicates this book to the esteemed James Thurber, who, it would seem, first ascertained and defined the Walter Mitty syndrome, a characteristic often found in the psyche of us Corvette owners who appear frequently to be confusing ourselves with Andretti, Foyt, and Fittipaldi.

The Author wishes to give thanks to the Owners of cars featured in this work. No attempt has been made to isolate the cars. Since we have been attempting to describe the *characteristics* of a given year, we have deliberately employed those pictures which best served the immediate purpose. *For this reason, adjacent photos may not necessarily show views of the same car.*

CONTENTS

cor-vette', 1 ker-vet'; 2 cŏr-vĕt', *n.* *Naut.* A flush-decked wooden war-vessel, generally equipped with only one tier of guns, resembling a frigate in being a full-rigged ship, and ranking next below it. In the United States called a *sloop of war.* [< F. *corvette,* < Sp. *corveta.* < L. *corbita.* < *corbis,* basket.] **cor'vett**.

Funk & Wagnild's New Standard Dictionary of the
English Language — 1942 Edition

Despite some minor variations in their definitions, (Webster's New Twentieth Century Dictionary adds "a slow-sailing ship of burden" as an alternate), dictionaries tend to agree that a "corvette" *is* a small naval vessel. Their view is supported by the authoritative Jane's *Pocket Book of Major Warships,* 1973 edition, which adds that ex-United States Corvettes are still in service. The navies of the Philipines presently have 5; South Vietnam, 3; South Korea, 8; Taiwan, 1; Cuba, 2; and Ecuador, also 2.

These ex-United States Navy Corvettes were built in 1942-44, were 185 feet long, displaced 640 tons and had a complement of 90 Officers and men. They had a top speed of 15 knots and were lightly armed with only one 3 inch gun and a few 20 mm anti-aircraft guns.

Urgencies of a situation sometimes cause a relaxation of the precise, and emotional ingredients frequently flavor a concept. So it was with the corvette which, due to its extensive service in convoy protection (where it was popularly believed to be capable of darting in and around the other vessels to engage, attack, and destroy the enemy submarines), survived the war with an unearned reputation best summed up in the words "youthful abandon, and dashing, quick, response".

So it was to be. Some ten years later, in 1953, Chevrolet selected the word to describe its new sports car.

Introduction

In the late 1940's, European-built "sports cars" were starting to trickle in to the United States in the hand of returning servicemen who had taken the opportunity while overseas to enjoy them. Chief among these early cars was the British MG whose small size, racy look, spartan appearance, short rear deck, and long boxy hood appeared in vivid contrast to the Detroit cars. Although underpowered, the MG with a characteristic rumble to its exhaust, brought forth a vision of tweed-jacketed, pipe-smoking Englishmen in checkered driving caps tooling around the Hedgerows. There was an undeniable *difference* between that car with its "sporting" driver, and the far more bulbous, larger, heavier, and less quick American-built sedan.

Not long after, the Jaguar also began to appear here. This car, with long flowing front fenders neatly melded into its two-seated body, improved on matters by actually *being* a racing car. With superb handling characteristics, excellent acceleration, good staying power, and road racing was now provided with a machine that *belonged*.

Placed on a turntable before a photo-mural of the New York skylines, the prototype Corvette appeared at the General Motors Motorama in January of 1953. As is common with such prototypes, styling changes were made prior to production. The downward-pointing "fin" on the sides was replaced with one pointing upwards, side trim extended to the rear fender well, hood (and deck lid) script eliminated, outside door buttons and fender air scoops removed, and the Chevrolet "bowtie" on the wheelcovers rotated to align with the "ears" of the spinners.

A photograph of the prototype Corvette taken early in 1953 shows the script nameplate on the rear deck which later was omitted in production.

Relatively few shared an active enthusiasm for the cars though (in 1952 there were fewer than 12,000 "sports cars" registered in the United States). There was, however, another factor. In 1948 Volkswagen had imported two cars; by 1952 they were to bring in over 150,000. If much of the buying public had apparently deceived itself into believing that it was getting a "sports car" when it acquired the frisky little "Bug", the fact remained that the American public *was* becoming more and more involved in imported cars, most of which were either two-seated or "sporty" or both.

By the early Fall of 1951, others had built domestic sports cars independently. None, however, was destined to become highly successful (even the fiber-glass body had been conceived and produced long before Chevrolet got into the act). As excellent as many of these early American sports cars may have been, *none* were to enjoy huge success. Equally, competing manufacturers were believed to be working on their own versions of such cars, and it is therefore not surprising that General Motors was also quietly considering such a vehicle.

General Motors' Styling Staff, a highly progressive group, had almost surreptitiously devoted limited time to the layouts of a small two-passenger sports type car intended as a response to the growing interest. By mid 1952, they had already produced a full size clay model of their as-yet-unnamed car.

Chevrolets of the early 1950's were distinguished neither by their advanced styling nor by overly exciting engineering. Full-bodied, somewhat drab, they were powered by a dependable, if sluggish, six cylinder engine. From a high of over 1,300,000 cars produced in 1950, Chevrolet's conservative image contributed to a decline in sales which saw 1952 barely clear 825,000 units, a loss of over half a million cars. Clearly *something*, perhaps *everything* had to be done, and done fast to attract the public's interest to General Motors. The 1953 models were already scheduled to have some improvements (the wrap-around windshield was introduced on the Chevrolet with that model), but almost *any* added project which would generate good publicity was sure to be approved.

Thus, when the clay-and-plaster model was presented to General Motors President, Harlow "Red" Curtice, ex-salesman under whose guidance the General Motors Motorama had been conceived, it was an immediate hit. Noting the publicity possibilities of such a display at the forthcoming 1953 Motorama, Curtice approved the project as a "dream car" display for the Chevrolet Division.

"Dream cars" were nothing new. Years never went by but that Styling Staff studies were made, considered, even built, in clay, plaster, chicken wire, etc. Most of these "dream cars" were to live comparatively short lives although certainly there were features of some of those studies which later found their way into the evolutionary growth of the conventional product.

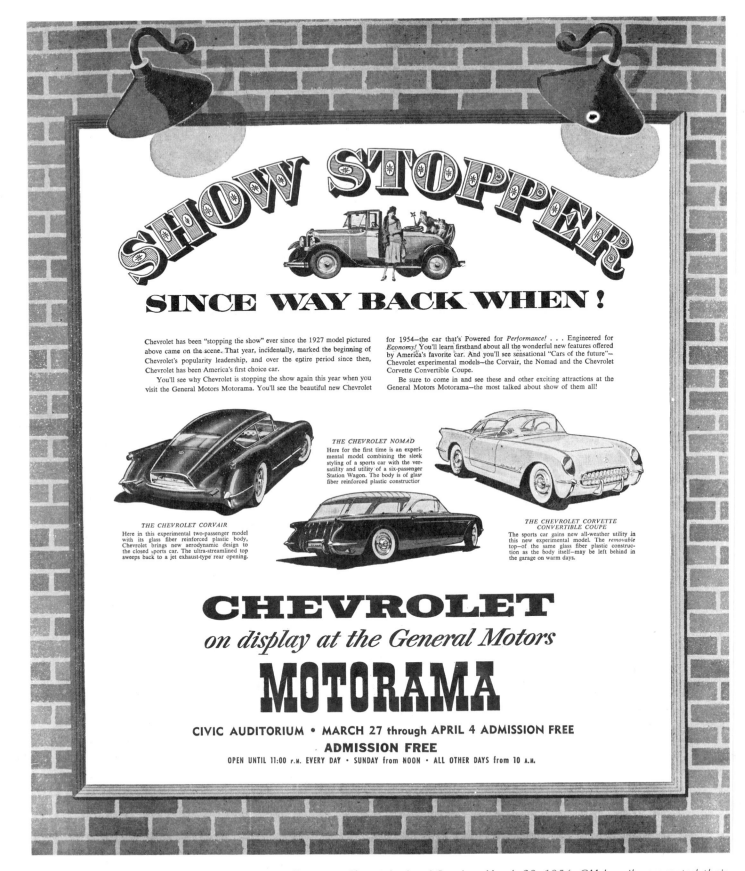

SHOW STOPPER

SINCE WAY BACK WHEN!

Chevrolet has been "stopping the show" ever since the 1927 model pictured above came on the scene. That year, incidentally, marked the beginning of Chevrolet's popularity leadership, and over the entire period since then, Chevrolet has been America's first choice car.

You'll see why Chevrolet is stopping the show again this year when you visit the General Motors Motorama. You'll see the beautiful new Chevrolet

for 1954—the car that's Powered for *Performance!* . . . Engineered for *Economy!* You'll learn firsthand about all the wonderful new features offered by America's favorite car. And you'll see sensational "Cars of the future"—Chevrolet experimental models—the Corvair, the Nomad and the Chevrolet Corvette Convertible Coupe.

Be sure to come in and see these and other exciting attractions at the General Motors Motorama—the most talked about show of them all!

THE CHEVROLET NOMAD
Here for the first time is an experimental model combining the sleek styling of a sports car with the versatility and utility of a six-passenger Station Wagon. The body is of glass fiber reinforced plastic construction

THE CHEVROLET CORVAIR
Here in this experimental two-passenger model with its glass fiber reinforced plastic body, Chevrolet brings new aerodynamic design to the closed sports car. The ultra-streamlined top sweeps back to a jet exhaust-type rear opening.

THE CHEVROLET CORVETTE CONVERTIBLE COUPE
The sports car gains new all-weather utility in this new experimental model. The *removable* top—of the same glass fiber plastic construction as the body itself—may be left behind in the garage on warm days.

CHEVROLET
on display at the General Motors
MOTORAMA

CIVIC AUDITORIUM • MARCH 27 through APRIL 4 ADMISSION FREE
ADMISSION FREE
OPEN UNTIL 11:00 P.M. EVERY DAY • SUNDAY from NOON • ALL OTHER DAYS from 10 A.M.

In a special 12 page supplement to the San Francisco Chronicle dated Sunday, March 28, 1954, GM heavily promoted their 1954 Motorama. Reproduced above is the Chevrolet Division's full page advertisement in that supplement. Feature stories included a report that Chevrolet was heavily concentrating on their Bel Air six-model series (expanded from the single hard top coupe of 1953) and a description of a trip-hammer destruction test of the Corvette's plastic body in which some 2000 blows per hour are rained on the body of the car with little apparent effect.

What was *this* "dream car"? A hastily contrived, incompletely conceived, radically departing, insufficiently powered, technologically advanced, and eccentrically styled "sports" car! Curiously though, as luck would have it, timing was right, the enthusiasm of the originators was high, and the apparent public reaction happily encouraging. Overlooking its faults, accepting its limitations, ignoring its problems, and worshipping its characteristic noise, the car was to be enveloped by its public.

* * * * *

General Motors' Motorama, a reportedly $1,500,000 show, was intended to stimulate public interest in the products of all *of its Divisions from Cadillac through Buick, Oldsmobile, Pontiac, and Chevrolet. Included too were the Frigidaire, Guide Lamp and GMC Truck Division. In 1953, amid 135 dazzling exhibits replete with attractive models, both human and automotive, the products were to be placed on display and the public invited (free admission) to attend in a carnival-like promotional atmosphere.*

The New York Times, on December 6, 1952, reported the plans for the GM Motorama to be held at the Waldorf-Astoria Hotel in January of the following year, but nothing in the announcement (or in most of the subsequent "news" reports) suggested the introduction at that show of the car that was to become one of the few Classics of recent times.

The Motorama opened in New York City with a luncheon preview for the Press on January 16th, 1953 followed by the public opening the following day. It was reported that over 45,000 people attended that first day. When the show closed six days later an enthusiastic report was made that "over 300,000" people had viewed the cars on display. Over $800,000 in sales volume was reported to have been written on the existing lines, and high interest on the part of potential Corvette buyers was noted. The Motorama then departed New York for similar showings in Miami, Chicago, Los Angeles, San Francisco, Dallas, and Kansas City.

* * * * *

That the Corvette was "hastily contrived" is obvious. In just under nine months from the time it was approved for the purpose, this "dream car" was brought from clay, paper, and plaster, to a full-size operating automobile. With an entirely new body, made of glass-reinforced polyester resins (selected largely to save the time and cost of making tooling for a conventional metal body), even an entirely new chassis had to be developed. Although production parts from other General Motors lines were employed wherever possible (i.e. door knobs were from the 1952 Cadillac as was the radio), the *sum* of the parts had to appear as an entirely new car.

Its "incomplete" conception is best illustrated by the discovery after assembly of the first unit that the glass body was not an electrical conductor and normal "gounding" of circuits had to be supplemented by a two-wire electrical system. Its "radical departure" is self-evident; how could a comparison be made between this beautiful little two-seater and a conventional sedan? It's "eccentric styling" was never more obvious than in a rain where, it was reported, "one could use the water leaks to extinguish cigarettes". Despite all of this, continuing reports of potential buyers clamoring for the car as it was shown around the country supported a decision to place the dream car in production. Thus it was that on July 1, 1953, the New York Times reported on the production the previous day of the first of 300 Corvettes to be produced by Chevrolet during the last half of 1953. On the first of January of 1954 production officially began at the St. Louis facility of the Division which has remained Corvette's home ever since.

The three dream cars of the 1954 Motorama, shown with the 1954 production Corvette are the removable hard-top with roll-up windows, a modification of a production car, the CORVAIR fast back coupe which was never produced, and a NOMAD prototype. While strongly resembling the Corvette in certain areas, the Nomad was actually built on a standard Chevrolet chassis, not that of a Corvette.

For 1954's Motorama, Styling was able to refine their earlier design even further. The lack of roll-up windows in the prototypes was corrected in the 1954 "dream car", and a smart new removable hard top was fashioned. (Neither of these two needed improvements however were to find their way into the 1954 or even 1955 Corvette.) In addition, Styling showed a "Fastback" version called the "Corvair", a name to be later used, in 1960 for their rear-engined economy car, and a highly styled two-door station wagon (built on a stock Chevy chassis) resembling the Corvette in fender and body panel treatments. This latter car was to later be produced, in modified form, and introduced in the 1955 Bel Air line.

With only about 350 cars under their belt, Chevrolet people were probably not yet prepared for the Ford "counter-attack", and must have been shocked when on February 20, 1954, Ford presented their response, the two-passenger Thunderbird, initially presented as a "sports car", but almost immediately redefined as a "personal car". With metal body, V-8 engine, roll-up windows, and a removable hard top, its long low lines a distinct contrast to Corvette's rounded appearance. Ford's small car sold over 16,000 units in 1955 while Chevrolet was hard pressed to find buyers for 4700.

It is a real example of determination to succeed that Chevrolet did not withdraw from the market at that time, but they did not, coming back in 1956 with a new model having windows, tops, and a V-8 engine. Despite this, again the Thunderbird substantially outsold the Corvette, and it was only with Ford's withdrawal from the two-seater market in 1958 (after they had produced and sold some 53,000 Thunderbirds) that Corvette again became Detroit's only two seated sports car.

Although in recent years, the Corvette has taken on the appearance of a "luxury car" with tilting and telescoping steering wheels, air conditioning, am/fm radios, soft cushioned seats, etc. it is the one distinctly American car that basically still handles properly. With quick responsive steering, high acceleration, smooth yet powerful engine, it, even now, offers the motoring public the opportunity to drive something just a bit "different". It is to Chevrolet's lasting credit that the Corvette was maintained in production.

By late 1954, sales were being stimulated by a series of ads extolling the Corvette. This one, appearing in the September issue of Motor Trend, reminds readers that the car is after all, available, and not just a dream car.

"The Marque of ZORA"

Zora Arkus-Duntov, often referred to as "Mr. Corvette", is an extraordinary man, a legendary figure throughout the entire automotive world. Born of Russian parents in Belgium, educated in the Soviet Union and Germany, Arkus-Duntov is one of the most remarkable engineers ever to work in Detroit. However, his career with General Motors cannot be explained solely in terms of his ability. Timing, audacity, and perserverence have also been key ingredients.

To know "Mr. Corvette", we must first know Zora Arkus-Duntov, At the time of his birth, Zora's father was an engineering student in Belgium, his mother a medical student who later looked after thousands of children orphaned by war and the revolution. Zora grew up in the capital of Czarist Russia, Petrograd, and attended the Petrograd Electro-Technical Institute. His first acquaintance with an American-made product was a Smith & Wesson revolver—used to fend off those who might steal his bread ration.

After obtaining a Mechanical Engineering degree in 1934, Duntov worked in Germany, Belgium, and France designing machine tools, superchargers, and diesel engines, and as World War II approached, even hand grenades. Unable to remain neutral, Zora joined the French Air Force, and after France surrendered, he made his way to Spain, Portugal, and on to the United States where he and his brother, Yura, operated a manufacturing company in New York. After the war, Zora and Yura designed and built the well-known Ardun (for Arkus-Duntov) heads which remain the most popular overhead valve conversion units ever built for the Ford "flathead" V-8 engines.

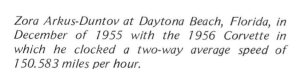

Zora Arkus-Duntov at Daytona Beach, Florida, in December of 1955 with the 1956 Corvette in which he clocked a two-way average speed of 150.583 miles per hour.

As a student in Germany, Zora had bought a motorcycle, and later an ancient 50 horsepower race car. From this beginning, he stepped into racing engine design and then racing cars himself. Over a span of almost three decades, he drove Grand Prix Talbots, Cisitalias, Allards, and Porsches. At Le Mans, he won class honors in a Porsche in 1954 and 1955; twice though he failed to finish in Allards. He set a Pikes Peak stock car record in 1955 in a pre-production 1956 Chevrolet and broke the then-existing production sports car flying mile record in a 1956 Corvette at Daytona Beach. His last race, however, was in a 250F Maserati in 1960 at Meadowbrook, near Chicago.

In the early 1950's, Duntov was serving as an engineering consultant to Sydney Allard, builder of the thundering Allard racing cars. Along with the thousands of others, he was able to view Corvette's debut at General Motors' Motorama at the Waldorf-Astoria in January of 1953. Favorably impressed by the car's appearance, he regarded it as "the prettiest sports car I had ever seen". Although he felt that the car, at the same time, was "a shell with no engine; no personality", he believed that the car had great potential and he *wanted* to work on it. His subsequent correspondence with Chevrolet resulted in an offer which he happily accepted, and he joined their Research & Development staff in May of 1953.

Only six weeks after joining Chevrolet, Zora asked for a leave of absence in order to race for Allard. Returning, he spent some 18 months working on advanced engineering projects of general interest, but in early 1955, Zora was instructed to "improve the driveability" of the coming 1956 Corvette and

In 1955 Zora set a stock car record in the Pikes Peak Hill Climb, an annual event instituted in 1916. He flashed up the 12½ mile course which rises almost a full mile to 14,110 feet in 17 minutes, 24.05 seconds in this pre-production 1956 Chevrolet. Asked if he had ever considered the possibility of skidding off the mountain, (below), he quickly replied "Never!". (Thirteen years later in another Chevrolet, this time with a 336 cid engine, Bobby Unser managed to reduce the time to just under 12 minutes.)

Sebring, Florida in 1957, and Zora was there to pilot the experimental Corvette SS. The vehicle, constructed of a special light weight magnesium alloy skin over a chrome-molybdenum tubular steel frame incorporated many experimental features in addition to its unusual construction. Among these were some that found their way into the production vehicles including fuel injection and a close-ratio 4-speed transmission.

to design wind-up windows to replace the removable plexiglass windows. The result was a better balanced suspension, improved handling, roll-up (and optionally powered) windows, and more headroom. The mark of Zora now in evidence, was soon to become the Marque of Zora, for, with the exception of the 1968 model which was designed when Zora was sidelined for an operation, every Corvette since bears "Mr. Corvette's" stamp of approval. He was assigned product responsibility for the Corvette engine and chassis in 1963, and was named Chief Corvette Engineer in 1968.

Each Corvette built during the past two decades is, in a way, a mobile monument to Duntov. As for his specific engineering achievements, they are so numerous as to defy a listing. Suffice it to say that he was the engineering genius responsible for putting many advanced items on the Corvette that later turned up on more conventional GM cars . . . fuel injection, disc brakes, retractable headlights, limited slip differentials, and the list goes on and on. Many advanced designs carried Duntov's imprint. The 1957 Corvette SS race car (now in the Indianapolis Speedway Museum) and the 1960 mid-engined, open-wheeled, single-seat CERV 1 are but two. (Readers interested in this facet of Corvette's history are referred to "Corvette, America's Star-Spangled Sports Car" by

Shown chatting in the mid-Fifties with international racing star Sterling Moss (center) and John Fitch, one of this country's great road-racing drivers, Zora listened intently to their views.

Karl Ludvigsen, an excellent work on that subject.) CERV 1, built as a research machine, was among other things a "test bed" for the four wheel independent suspension design later found on the 1963 Sting Ray.

As Duntov reflects on his Corvette years, he observes that timing has played an important role in his career. He was ready for the Corvette when the 'Vette was ready for him; Ford moved away from the two-seat Thunderbird with the 1958 model, and Chevrolet decided to move ahead with, rather than bury the Corvette. "We saw Ford's move away from the two-seater as a great opportunity" recalls Duntov, "and believed that we could take over the place it was vacating. At that time, I believed that we could boost Corvette production from 700 in 1955 to 20,000 or more and that we should plan our productive capacity accordingly. But nobody seemed to share my belief in those days".

Shifts in GM's racing policies affected his work, as did Chevrolet's periodic changes in Management. Detroit's love-hate attitude toward racing might have defeated a lesser man than Duntov. During most of his GM career he worked with Executives who were at least tolerant, if not enthusiastic, about racing, but GM's top management was plainly negative about the sport. Corporate officials merely asked themselves "how many cars will it sell?" Thus Chevrolet and Dutov were *openly* associated with racing only until 1957 when the Automobile Manufacturers Association banned factory participation in "speed contests".

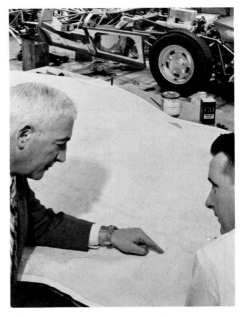

In less glamorous surroundings, engineer Arkus-Duntov checks blueprints for accuracy. Commencing with his design work on the 1956 Corvette, he continued with the car and was assigned full product responsibility for the engine and chassis in 1963 and was named Chief Corvette Engineer in 1968, a post that he held until his retirement at the end of 1974.

CERV-1, Chevrolet Experimental Racing Vehicle, built and tested in the early 1960's incorporated innovations such as a mid-engined chassis, an all-aluminum engine including block, heads, and most accessories, which weighed almost 90 pounds less than the stock engine, and independent rear suspension that would find its way into the 1963 'Vette. Here piloted by Duntov on the test track, the name was later altered to minimize the intent and the vehicle is now known as Chevrolet Engineering Research Vehicle.

Reflectively contemplating a model of a mid-engined Corvette which incorporated a rotary engine, Duntov describes GM's decision not to produce the vehicle as the "only major disappointment in his long career.

In 1962, Ford re-entered racing, noting in doing so that the AMA resolution had been interpreted "more and more freely". Duntov had hope that GM would do the same, but this was not to be. So Zora quietly continued until the late 1960's to "improve the Corvette's performance" and on occasion to "loan" hot Corvettes to selected race drivers and teams. When Duntov showed up at Daytona or Sebring with special Corvettes for trials and was asked why he was there, he would reply blandly "Many of our customers race, and we therefore feel a responsibility to know our product's limitations under racing conditions".

Duntov's greatest disappointment, in fact his only "major disappointment" to use his words was the Company's decision not to produce the mid-engine Corvette. He fought hard for this vehicle, and at times is seemed within his grasp. Finally, in 1973, he was told that the car was not to be produced thus ending the project for him. The present Corvette was enjoying a satisfactory level of sales, and the high cost of tooling an entirely new model could not be considered for at least another five years. Retired at the end of December of 1974, Duntov was thus to be barred from working on an all-new Corvette, and he turned his attention to the study of "super-efficient" engines. As he sees it, the fuel crisis has heightened the need for research into engines that display not only performance, but also high efficiency.

Today Arkus-Duntov enjoys his life as a resident of one of Detroit's most fashionable suburbs. Surrounded by mementos of his engineering and racing careers, he has more books and magazines than he has time to read, and he still manages to get out to the GM Technical Center on a fairly regular basis. Nowadays he is again enthusiastic about airplanes, and intends to buy one and resume his flying. If one thing seems certain, it is that he will remain active, seeking again to place his special mark of achievement as he did on the Corvette, truly the "Marque of Zora".

January 1975, and now retired, Zora Arkus-Duntov for twenty years the man who made it what it was, can justly enjoy his marque.

1953

sensational styling

amazing acceleration

extra-low center of gravity

outstanding performance

The Thrilling New Chevrolet Corvette
THE FIRST ALL-AMERICAN SPORTS CAR!

This Folder, distributed in 1953, incorporates the Prototype rather than the production models in its illustrations.

Originally printed on glossy paper, rough finish in this photo indicates a reproduction.

SPORTS CAR PRODUCED
Chevrolet Corvette Has Body of Laminated Glass Fiber

Special to The New York Times.

FLINT, Mich., June 30—The first production model Chevrolet corvette sports car, with a laminated glass fiber body, was completed here today.

It has been priced at $3,250 f. o. b., including Powerglide automatic transmission. T. H. Keating, general manager of the General Motors, Chevrolet Division, said that the company planned to build fifty corvettes a month in the remainder of the 1953 model year.

"We expect to complete our original schedule of 300 corvettes in this model year," he added.

Two experimental models of the new sports car have been displayed in auto shows across the country. The car stands only 33 inches off the road. It is a two seater, 70 inches wide, 167 inches long and has a 102-inch wheelbase. The curb weight of the corvette is approximately 2,900 pounds.

The first 300 Corvettes were all painted Polo White and were trimmed in Sportsman Red and White interiors and Black tops. They were virtually hand-made and consequently exhibited a tendency to vary somewhat.

In their edition of July 1, 1953, the New York Times dutifully reported the initial assembly of Chevrolet's sports car. Off-handedly dismissed with lower case spelling, Corvette's birth was noted on that newspaper's obituary page.

In later years, CORVETTE NEWS, Chevrolet's highly regarded publication, attempted to locate the first Corvette produced. The earliest one found is the third car, a tracing of whose data plate is reproduced here. Owned by Ed Thiebaud of Creston, California, the car stands as the oldest remaining Corvette unless, and until, the two earlier models are located.

The 1953 Corvette

Although it had already been decided that their new Corvette car would be produced in their St. Louis Assembly plant, the urgency suggested by public interest in the car at the Motorama caused Chevrolet to advance their plans. A limited run was to be produced where initial manufacturing "bugs" could be worked out promptly, where engineering changes could most expeditiously be incorporated, and where development and experimental knowledge could be most closely coordinated. Thus, 300 units, essentially "pre-production" models would be completed in Flint, Michigan, before scheduled high-rate production commenced in St. Louis in January of 1954.

At Flint, each car was serially numbered, starting with the initial designation of E53F001001, with the following cars carrying sequentially numbered data plates through the last of the 300 in December of 1953. In January, St. Louis production lines repeated the designations starting with their first car, E54S001001.

Preceeding the serial number on early data plates is thus the added information "E53F". This indicates Corvette (E), 1953 production (53), and Flint assembly (F), and explains the subsequent derivation of the term "1953 Corvette". By that name is meant those 300 cars produced at Flint in the last half of the calendar year of 1953.

Chevrolet did not promote the car as a "1953 Corvette", and the "1954" and the "1953" Corvettes are properly treated as a single model, the initial one. Despite variations of relatively minor nature, (almost invariably the result of "running" type changes), the *principal* difference between the so-called "1953 Corvette" and the "1954" model is the serial number plate.

A well-circulated photograph, taken in the Flint assembly plant, possibly for promotional purposes, shows a "production" crew of six men and a draftsman completing the assembly of early Corvettes. Fitted with 1953 Chevrolet Bel Air dress-up wheel covers (right), perhaps due to an unexplained absence of the planned unique covers, this photograph infers that perhaps some of the earliest Corvettes were so equipped, but there appears to be little other supporting evidence.

Chevrolet Corvette for 1954
The First All-American Sports Car

SPECIFICATIONS

POWER-PACKED CHASSIS

ENGINE—"Blue-Flame 150," 150-horsepower, high-compression, 6-cylinder valve-in-head engine; three side-draft carburetors, shielded ignition, dual exhaust system, reserve water tank.

TRANSMISSION—Powerglide; with floor-mounted selector lever.

DRIVE LINE—Hotchkiss drive; 3.55 to 1 ratio, hypoid axle.

WHEELS—Five steel wheels; full-size chrome disks with simulated hubs. Five 6.70-15 white sidewall tires.

STEERING—16 to 1 ratio, anti-friction gear; Center-Point linkage. Nearly vertical, 17¼", two-spoke steering wheel.

BRAKES—Hydraulic, 11", self-energizing brakes; bonded linings. Mechanical parking brakes; pull-handle and alarm light.

SUSPENSION—Knee Action with ride stabilizer; outrigger type, 51", 4-leaf rear springs. Direct double-acting shock absorbers.

FRAME—Extra-rigid, X-member-braced Box Girder frame.

GAS TANK—17 gallons; behind seats. Concealed filler at side.

LIGHTWEIGHT BODY

BODY—2-passenger, open-cockpit body of glass-fiber reinforced plastic; light, strong, durable, rustproof, quiet and easy to repair. Wide doors with inside release lever.

COMPARTMENTS — Front-hinged hood with automatically latching support. Large luggage locker with spare wheel well under floor, and lockable, counter-balanced lid. Concealed well for top in rear deck behind seats. Saddle-covered door pockets.

WINDOWS AND TOP—Chrome-bound, one-piece, curved safety plate glass windshield; 53-degree slant. Removable, chrome-bound, plastic side windows with ventipanes. Manually adjusted fabric top with plastic rear window.

COLORS—Exterior: Polo White. Cockpit: Sportsman Red seat and side wall upholstery; red-crowned, white instrument panel; red carpet. Luggage Locker: Sportsman Red. Top: Tan.

★ ★ ★

CAR DIMENSIONS—Wheelbase, 102". Length, 167". Height, 33" at door top. Road Clearance, 6". Width, 70". Tread, 57" front, 59" rear. Curb Weight, 2850 lb. Weight Distribution, 53% front, 47% rear. Body Weight, 410 lb.

In an early folder, the Corvette for 1954 was presented as "The First All-American Sports Car". Its agile performance was explained by its great engine power combined with the light plastic body and small size. New in style was the smooth flowing streamlined look with rounded lines and carefully concealed lights, hinges, and other usual projections, including the customary protruding bumpers. Form-fitting seats (not yet called "bucket seats") with foam rubber padding and vinyl covering sharply differed from conventional bench type seats found in standard cars, and the Powerglide transmission shift lever was returned to the floor and joined by a utilitarian instrument panel to add to the sports car atmosphere. Despite this, "luxury" features *were* emphasized. The doors were provided with stowage compartments, a horn ring was standard, as were courtesy lights, windshield washers, and directional signals thus allowing an added claim of "luxurious comfort".

Early in 1954, colors besides the initial Polo White were introduced. These included Sportsman Red, Pennant Blue, and Corvette Copper. During 1954, the early black canvas top was replaced by a tan one.

1954 Corvette

Mr. Donald Yerkes, Carlsbad, California

1954

This insignia, appearing for the first time is again used on the 1955 model.

A radical new treatment of the headlights finds them recessed behind a protective chromed wire screen.

The distinctive frontal treatment of the early Corvettes is highlighted by an impressive 13-tooth chromed grill which continued in use through the 1957 model.

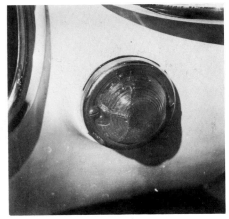

Parking lights are placed low and just outside the grill opening.

15" wheels are fitted with standard 6.70 x 15 whitewall tires and wheelcovers.

The highly polished, chromed covers are styled with two-eared "spinners", and the Chevrolet "bow tie" appears at the hub.

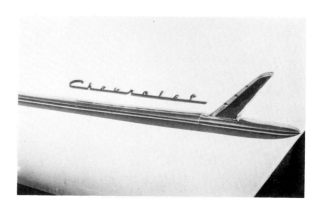

A flat pot-metal script nameplate appears on each fender. The "fin" portion of the side trim separates from the longer strip making a total of four sections in this stripe.

The side trim extends to the rear fender well, and by extending rear bumpers around the side, stripe is made to appear longer than it is.

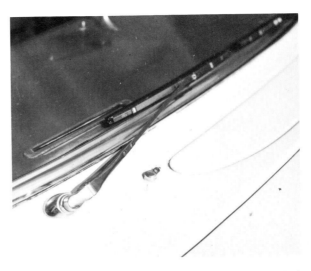

Dual windshield wipers are each fitted with a wind-shield washer nozzle as standard equipment. The cowl ventilator is opened by handle under the instrument panel.

The rakish lines of the car are emphasized by a sharply tilted (53º) safety plate glass windshield. Passenger cars had a sharply more erect windshield.

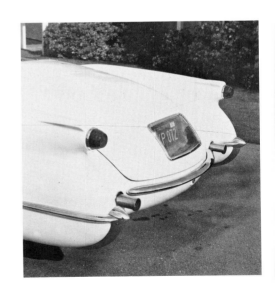

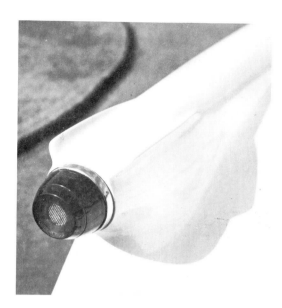

Fluted fins emphasize the protruding tail light pods, a new styling innovation this year.

Dual exhausts exit through the body on either side of of the center bumper section.

Rear fender guards are these chrome bumpers which extend both around the sides of the fender, and also beneath.

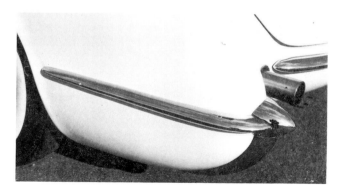

The lid latch is secured to its lower edge.

A counter-balanced rear deck lid opens to reveal limited storage space. Molded into this lid is a wire screen which serves as the radio antenna.

Beneath the center bumper bar is a lock for the rear deck lid.

All Corvettes were delivered with a black canvas top until well in to 1954 at which time a change was made to tan.

A recessed license plate is protected by a clear plastic window rimmed by a chromed frame.

A "Sportsman Red" rubber mat protects the floor of the luggage compartment, and bears a molded-in part number.

The removable plastic side windows (page 50) are stored in a vinyl compartmented bag which is secured to the forward wall of the compartment.

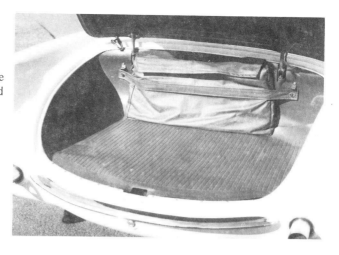

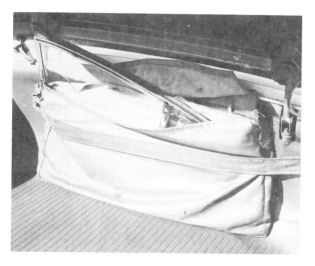

Two familiar Murphy fasteners hold the side window storage bag in place.

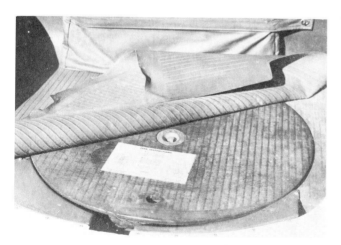

The spare tire is concealed beneath a removable floor section which is reached by removing the rubber floor mat.

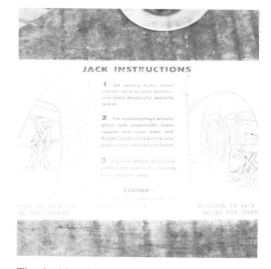

The jacking instruction sheet calls for jack to be placed under the rear axle or outer ends of front wheel supports. The car was not to be jacked on its bumpers.

The soft top, when erected, forms a curved profile. Rear window was not zippered.

These fittings, secured to the hatch cover, provide an anchor point for the soft top when erected.

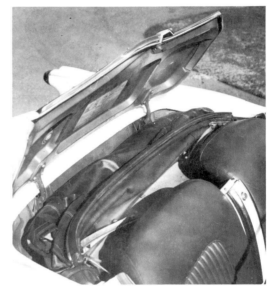

The driver's seat back is extended deeply to permit the seat to be adjusted forward and still fall under the lid.

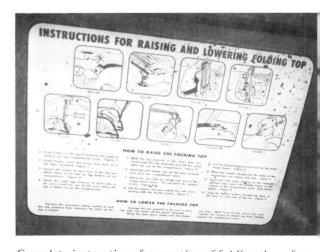

Complete instructions for erecting of folding the soft top are placed on the underside of the lid.

An outside rear view mirror is standard equipment on the car. Made by the Guide Division of GM, their name appears on the back of the mirror at the hub.

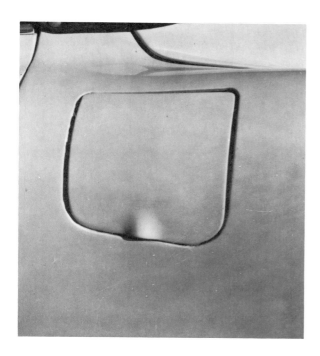

A large 17 gallon gasoline tank is placed behind the seats and reached through a filler tube under a spring-loaded hatch on the left rear fender.

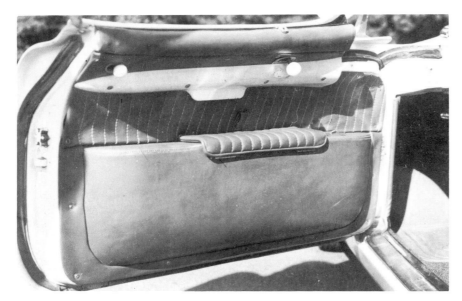

Just below the courtesy light switch on the left cowl is the identifying serial number plate for the car.

Wide doors provide attractive entry to the interior.

An ash tray is placed in each door.

White plastic knobs (which will persist until 1963) are used on the inside door release lever. There is no outside door handle or latch release.

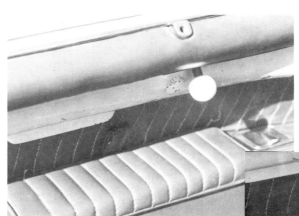

A storage compartment is provided in each door and protected with a snap-fastened cover.

The lines of the body are carried down between the seats to provide additional separation between them.

This button-operated latch secures the lid beneath which is stored the folded soft top.

The wide wrap-around windshield and the low-placed seats combine to provide a feeling of containment for the passengers.

The white instrument panel is red-topped for a most pleasing effect in which the cockpit colors are extended to the base of the windshield. An inside rear-view mirror is mounted on the instrument panel.

A 140 mph speedometer is calibrated some 20 miles per hour higher than the conventional passenger cars of the day adding to the suggestions of speed.

Beneath the speedometer is a warning light which is illuminated if parking brake is applied.

The instrument panel is white, but with substantial red trim. The cowl panels are stitched as is the door, and is also covered in red vinyl. The steering wheel is disc-shaped, and its spokes are red (as is the steering column to its base) but the rim is white.

The horn-blowing ring, standard equipment, covers a larger quadrant than the 180° of the steering wheel spokes.

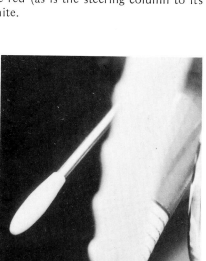

Directional signals are standard. A ribbed white plastic knob is used on the control lever.

The protruding edge of the instrument panel is padded. Beneath a hump in the surface is the radio speaker.

A rear view mirror is mounted at the center of the instrument panel.

Powerglide automatic transmission was standard in the early Corvette and no other transmission option was offered. The knob on the floor-mounted shift lever is lettered to indicate gear range, but no additional illumination is provided.

Suspended below the instrument panel is a white knob-tipped handle for the cowl ventilator. Sponge rubber-backed red carpet is placed on the floor.

The ignition lock on the left is followed by a fuel gauge, temperature gauge (beneath which is seen the cowl ventilator handle), and a tachometer in the center, below the radio. The tachometer not only indicates engine rpm, but records total revolutions since new.

To the right of the tachometer is an ammeter, oil pressure gauge, and an electric clock.

Initially fitted with a foot-operated pump, by 1954 the windshield washer system had been changed to a dual-function knob control.

Beneath the hood, and behind this grill, is the radio speaker. The lower segments of the grill are painted white to match the instrument panel. At its center appears the familiar Chevrolet crest.

Three side-draft carburetors are employed, but with space at a premium, they are fed through a manifold having only two air cleaners.

The top of the two-piece air filter is chromed.

Carter side-draft carburetors are used.

Beneath the hood is the improved performance "Blue Flame 150", Chevrolet's reliable six cylinder engine refined to produce a rated 150 horsepower.

The carburetors are linked for parallel operation.

The front-hinged engine compartment cover is held in the open position by a sliding locking support at the front left side of the car.

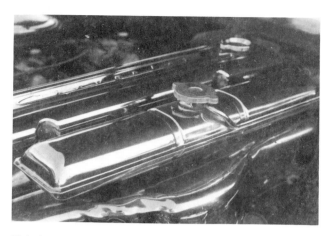

This is a radiator coolant reservoir placed longitudinally on the right side of the engine to enable a lower radiator. Beneath it is the windshield washer reservoir which was standard equipment on this car.

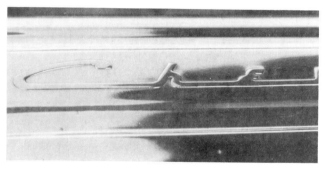

Earlier Corvettes had blue-green painted valve covers with the words "Blue Flame" painted on them. Later the covers were replaced with chromed steel valve covers bearing the word "Chevrolet".

Beneath the coolant tank is a metal shield placed over the spark plugs to shield radio frequency ignition noise as the plastic body will not do so as on metal cars.

Hydraulic brakes are operated by this master cylinder mounted on the firewall.

An ingenious removable side window with plastic panes is standard equipment. The entire frame can be detached and stored in the luggage compartment. (page 39).

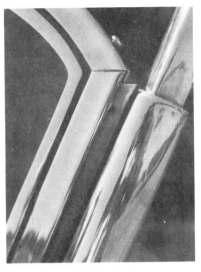

A rubber gasket seals the removable side window to the windshield.

A feature of the side windows is the vent pane which must be opened for access to the interior door release knob.

Information on the Plexiglas pane indicates that it was manufactured in June of 1954.

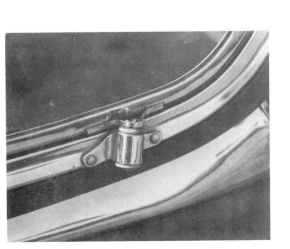

This is the lower hinge of the vent pane.

This sliding latch, operated either from the outside or the inside of the car, secures the vent pane.

The removable window assembly is then secured with this chromed thumb screw threaded into the receptacle in the door (below). The inside door knob is located where it can be easily reached through the unlockable vent pane.

The forward edge of the removable assembly has a pin which enters a hole in the windshield frame, a second pin fits into another hole at the base of the windshield, and a third enters a hole in the trim rail near the rear of the door.

" . . . . . A Cyclone of Power"

New 195-h.p.
Chevrolet
Corvette

V8

A brilliant new edition
of America's most popular
production sports car

SPECIFICATIONS

POWER-PACKED CHASSIS

ENGINES — Choice of 195-h.p. "Turbo-Fire V8" with 4-barrel carburetor; or 155-h.p. "Blue-Flame" Six with 3 side-draft carburetors. Valve-in-head design, 8:1 compression ratio, high-lift camshaft, dual exhaust system, shielded ignition.

TRANSMISSION — Powerglide Automatic Transmission. Floor-mounted selector lever.

DRIVE LINE — Hotchkiss drive. Hypoid axle: 3.55:1 with Powerglide Automatic Transmission.

TIRES — Five 6.70-15 tubeless tires.

STEERING — Anti-friction gear, 16 to 1 ratio; balanced linkage. Nearly vertical, 17¼" two-spoke steering wheel.

BRAKES — Hydraulic, 11" self-energizing brakes; bonded linings. Pull-handle parking brake.

SUSPENSION — Independent front suspension, ride stabilizer. Four-leaf rear springs, outrigger mounted. Direct double-acting shock absorbers.

FRAME — Extra-rigid X-member-braced box girder frame.

FUEL TANK — Capacity: 17 gal. Concealed side filler.

LIGHTWEIGHT BODY

BODY — 2-passenger, open-cockpit body of glass-fiber-reinforced plastic; light, strong, durable, quiet, rustproof, and easy to repair. Wide doors with inside release.

COMPARTMENTS — Front-hinged hood with automatically latching support. Large luggage locker with spare-wheel well under floor, and lockable counterbalanced lid. Concealed well for top in rear deck behind seats. Saddle-covered door pockets.

WINDOWS AND TOP — Chrome-bound, one-piece, curved safety plate glass windshield; 53-degree slant. Removable chrome-bound plastic side windows with ventipanes. Manually adjusted fabric top with plastic rear window.

COLORS — Exterior: Polo White or Pennant Blue. Cockpit: Sportsman Red or Beige seat and side wall upholstery; red- or blue-crowned white instrument panel; red or beige carpet. Luggage Locker: Sportsman Red or Beige. Top: Tan.

★   ★   ★

CAR DIMENSIONS — Wheelbase, 102". Length, 167". Height, 33" at door top. Road Clearance, 6". Width, 70". Tread, 57" front, 59" rear.

With much proudly to claim, Chevrolet nevertheless had to accept the criticisms leveled against their car. Although the public's reservation regarding the fiber-glass body had much to do with it, the fact that the car was underpowered with its six cylinder engine compounded their problems. The body could not be easily changed, but the engine could, and was. Commencing in 1955, Chevrolet's new V-8 found its way into Corvette, and although initially still only available with the Powerglide transmission, the fact that the new 195 hp engine was a V-8 may have been the turning point, for with 30% more horsepower to talk about, Corvette could properly claim . . . "A Cyclone of Power".

Other changes of note were the introduction of the 12 volt electrical system and an optional improved six now rated at 155 horsepower. Few of the 1955 were so equipped however, but late in the year a few cars were equipped with a 3-speed transmission. Sales of Corvette lagged and only 700 cars were produced in the entire model year making it the lowest production model in the series.

Colors for 1955 were Polo White exterior with red interior, Gypsy Red (a different shade than Sportsman Red), Corvette Copper with beige, and Harvest Gold (yellow) with green interior and although an early flyer for 1955 indicates that the Pennant Blue was carried forward from 1954, this is not believed to have been the case.

1955

1955 Corvette

Mr. David Graham, Westminster, California

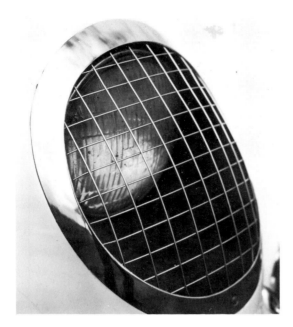

New 12 volt sealed beam lamps are again concealed behind the protective wire screen.

The 1955 frontal view is unchanged from that of 1954.

Eleven of these chromed steel "teeth" (plus two shorter ones at the ends) are assembled to provide the characteristic Corvette front grill.

Unchanged from 1954, the front bumpers again extend protectively downwards and around the sides of the fenders.

Although the housings are unchanged, parking light bulbs, like all others on the car, had to be changed to 12 volt ratings.

A distinguishing change in the side trim of the 1955 model is a subtle reminder of the initial use of the V-8 engine this year.

The forward "fin" is unchanged from last year.

This large gold-finished letter "V" is added *over* the earlier script.

The beautiful Corvette one-piece wrap-around windshield was a manufacturing triumph for the day. Although one-piece curved windshields were used on passenger cars, they did not extend around the sides as did this one.

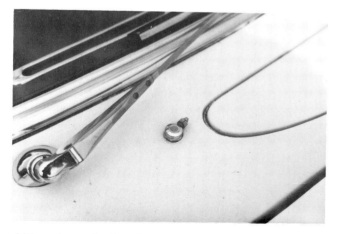

Although continuing the windshield washer as standard equipment, the 1955 model was again fitted with the original foot-operated pump unlike 1954 which employed a vacuum system.

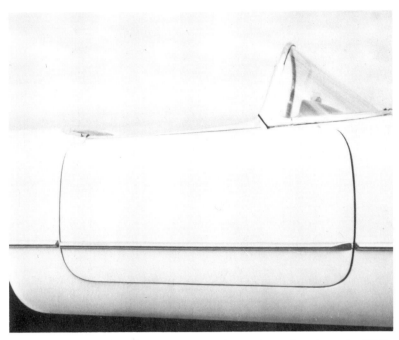

No outside door handles appear on the early series through 1955, and the sides of the cars are smooth, broken only by the lines of the wide doors. The chrome stripe (previous page) continues to the fender well.

A cleanly radiused wheel housing is emphasized by the standard 6:70 x 15 wide white wall tires. The apparent continuation of the side stripe behind the wheel housing is actually the extension of the rear bumper.

The Chevrolet "bowtie" insignia appears at the hub of the unique Corvette wheel covers.

Corvette's luggage compartment, while not overly large, is quite adequate since the spare tire is contained in a well beneath the deck.

A clear plastic cover is placed over the license plate set into the rear deck lid. Inbedded in the lid is a wire screen which serves as the radio antenna.

Podded tail lights are a styling innovation emphasized by the use of aerodynamic fins for still better effect.

A dual exhaust system (for both the new V-8 and also the six) extends through the body at the sides of the rear deck.

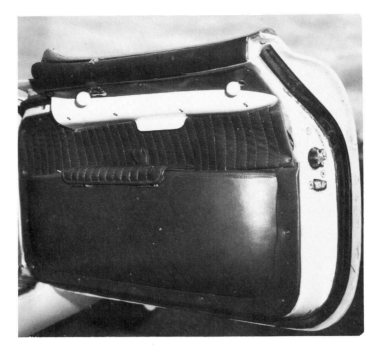

Interior trim on the door is unchanged from 1954 (page 42) and again exhibits distinctive saddle stitching. Small white knob at the left operates the door release. The matching knob on the right releases a spring-lock employed to secure the removable side windows.

The convenient storage compartments are again furnished in the doors.

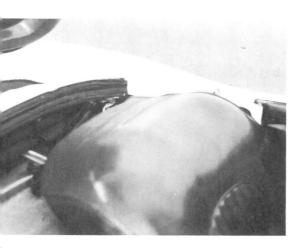

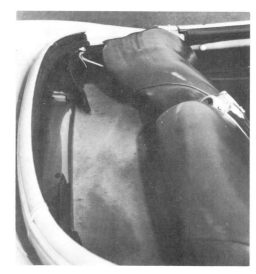

The soft top, furnished as standard equipment, folds neatly into a well behind the seats.

Wide back-rest at the top of the drivers seat is to allow it still to fall under the compartment cover when the seat is moved forward.

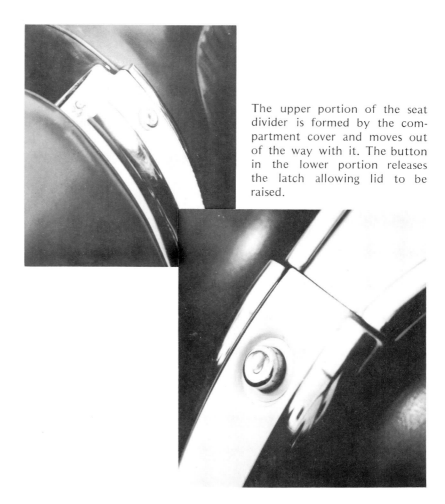

The upper portion of the seat divider is formed by the compartment cover and moves out of the way with it. The button in the lower portion releases the latch allowing lid to be raised.

The individual bucket seats are form-fitting with foam rubber cushioning, and the seams are saddle-stitched.

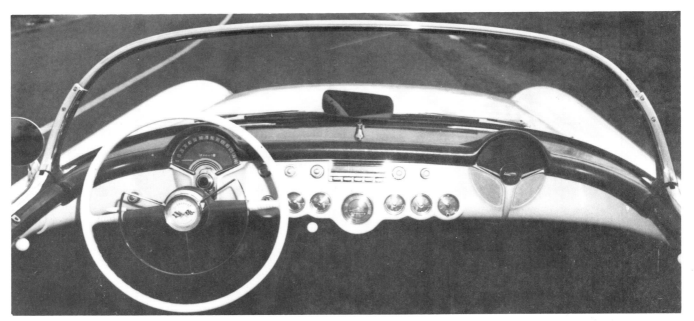

Highly attractive, and seemingly well balanced, the instruments are, in fact, rather difficult to see due to their location. The inside rear view mirror, on the other hand, offers excellent visibility.

1955 steering wheels were offered in several colors, beige and white, bronze and white, green and gold, and beige and red (first color refers to the spokes, second to the rim) to match the interiors. The color on the spokes extends down the steering column housing into the engine compartment.

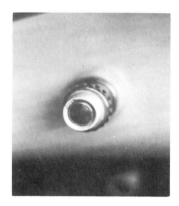

Headlight switch is located at left side of the instrument panel.

The speedomer is unchanged from 1954.

Although apparently identical with the earlier radio, 1955 brought a new model due to the change-over to a 12 volt electrical system.

ignition switch   fuel level   temperature   tachometer*   ammeter   oil pressure   clock

The tachometer is now calibrated to 6000 rpm.

Under the hood of the 1955 Corvette appears a new power plant, the 195 horsepower 265 cubic inch V-8 engine fitted with a four barrel carburetor. Boasting 8:1 compression ratio and a high lift camshaft, the engine was a smooth running unit which Chevrolet announced was carefully counter-balanced _after_ assembly.

The tachometer on the instrument panel is driven from a gear train at the back of the generator, not the engine itself.

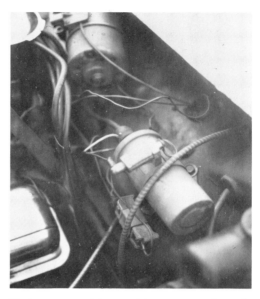

Tachometer drive cable passes through the firewall behind the left-side valve cover.

Distributor radio frequency shielding, a requirement with the non-shielding fiber-glass body, is achieved in several variations. This, for the 1955 V-8 engine is unique to that year.

A tube conducts heat from the exhaust manifold to the automatic choke on the carburetor.

"Action is the Keynote"

A NEW CORVETTE BY CHEVROLET

Now even greater than the original in . . .

Looks and Performance!

SPECIFICATIONS

ENGINE—Super-efficient valve-in-head design, 265-cubic-inch displacement, 3.75" bore x 3.0" stroke, 9.25 to 1 compression ratio. 210 horse-power at 5200 rpm and 270 foot-pounds of torque at 3200 rpm with single 4-barrel carburetor; 225 horsepower at 5200 rpm and 270 foot-pounds of torque at 3600 rpm with twin 4-barrel carbure-tors*. Special high-lift camshaft, high-speed valve system with mechanical lifters, special valve springs and spring dampers. Buffed, deep-ribbed cast aluminum rocker covers. Buffed aluminum racing-type oil-wetted air cleaners, special intake manifold. Full-pressure lubrication system with vertically mounted full-flow oil filter. High-power exhaust headers and full dual exhaust system. Full-circle, full-depth cylinder wall cooling, high-efficiency radiator, four-bladed slow-speed fan. Shielded ignition, 12-volt electrical system. Engine precision balanced after assembly.
TRANSMISSION—Choice of special high-perform-ance 3-speed close-ratio Synchro-Mesh (2.2:1 low and reverse, 1.31:1 second, 1:1 high) with high-capacity 10.5-inch coil-spring clutch, or optional Powerglide special automatic transmission.* Floor-mounted gear or range selector.
DRIVE SYSTEM—Hotchkiss drive, with unit-bal-anced tubular propeller shaft and universal joints.

REAR AXLE—High torque capacity axle; with Powerglide, 3.55:1 ratio; with Synchro-Mesh, 3.70:1 standard, 3.27:1 optional.
FRAME—Extra-rigid, welded box girder frame rein-forced with I-beam "X"-member.
SUSPENSION—Independent coil front suspension with ride stabilizer. Self-lubricating, semi-elliptic, four-leaf rear springs, outrigger mounted. Direct double-acting shock absorbers mounted inside coil springs on front and diagonally mounted on rear.
STEERING—Full anti-friction steering gear with 16:1 ratio and balanced steering linkage, 16:1 overall ratio. Competition-type steering wheel with 17" diameter and three shock-absorbing spring-steel spokes. Turning diameter (curb to curb), 36.55 feet right, 36.93 feet left.
BRAKES—Hydraulic 11-inch self-energizing brakes with new bonded linings, suspended brake pedal and readily accessible dash-mounted master cyl-inder. Total effective lining area, 158 square inches. Pull-handle parking brake mounted under left side of instrument panel operates rear brakes through independent mechanical linkage.
TIRES—Choice of black or white sidewall* stand-ard 6.70-15 4-ply tubeless. Spare tire concealed below floor of luggage compartment.

WHEEL COVERS—Full-diameter, chrome-plated with 10-spoke pattern and simulated knock-off hubs.
FUEL TANK—Filler cap concealed in left fender. 16.4-gallon tank contains filtering element for dirt and moisture protection.
EXTERIOR FEATURES—Glass-fibre-reinforced plas-tic with sculptured side panels; light, strong, dur-able, quiet, rustproof, easy to repair. Distinctive embossed hood, front hinged, with automatic support, inside release. Simulated twin fender air scoops. Two-passenger compartment, large luggage locker with spare-wheel well under floor, concealed top well behind seats. Unique Corvette crossed-flag emblems on hood and trunk lid. Twin exhaust ports integral with rear bumpers. Chrome-bound, one-piece, curved safety plate glass wind-shield. Choice of manually operated fabric top or light-weight easily removable plastic hardtop. Power operation* and hardtop* also optional with fabric top.
INTERIOR FEATURES—Form-fitting vinyl-covered seats, individually adjustable, with safety belt*. Wide doors with built-in arm rest, pushbutton door handle, key lock, inside door release, swing-out door hinges. Choice of crank-operated or power* window lifts. Ash tray and glove compart-ment between seats; simulated roll on instrument panel and doors, rubber-backed carpeting, metal door kick panels, sills, and step plates. Speed-ometer, tachometer, ammeter, and fuel level, oil pressure, and coolant temperature gauges. Signal-seeking radio*, heater*, directional signals, electric clock, cigarette lighter, outside and inside rear-view mirror, windshield washer*.
COLORS—Onyx Black or Onyx Black and Silver with Red interior and Black or White top, Venetian Red or Venetian Red and Beige with Red interior and Beige or White top, Cascade Green or Cas-cade Green and Beige with Beige interior and Beige or White top, Aztec Copper or Aztec Copper and Beige with Beige interior and Beige or White top, Arctic Blue or Arctic Blue and Silver with Red or Beige interior and Beige or White top, Polo White or Polo White and Silver with Red interior and White or Black top.
DIMENSIONS—Wheelbase, 102". Length, 168.0". Overall height: top down, 49.2"; Convertible top, 51.1"; hardtop, 51.0". Height at door 33.0". Road clearance 6". Width, 70.5". Tread, 57" front, 59.3" rear.

*Optional at extra cost.

1956 saw a new model unveiled with a more pleasing shape highlighted by a sweeping side trim that was to become a Corvette identification for several years. Chevrolet's three-speed transmission was standard although Powerglide was an option, as was a dual carburetor higher performance engine in place of the standard 4-barrel carburetor set-up. Earlier, in Sebring, Florida, Corvette had won its class in the Production Sports Car class, and had shown well in the grueling 12 hour Grand Prix race to gain prominence in racing circles. Thus, this newly acquired reputation established that for 1956, "Action is the Keynote".

1956 Corvette

Mr. Bob Wingate, Glendora, California

New frontal treatment is distinguished principally by revised headlights.

New hood ornament contains a stylized feature often associated with the letter V as in V-8.

Sealed beam headlights are now mounted forward on the fenders and trimmed with an encircling chromed frame.

The characteristic 13 tooth grill is retained as is the oval trim surrounding it.

Parking lights, while unchanged in style, have been moved to a more protected area behind the bumpers which have themselves been simplified.

A new bumper again curls around sides of the fender, but does not have the vertical portion which was removed to make room for parking light.

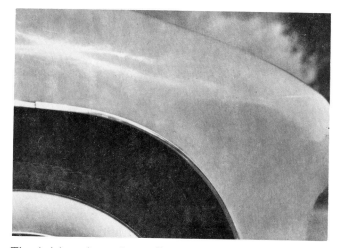

The bright trim strip outlines the front wheel housing and continues to border the insert panel.

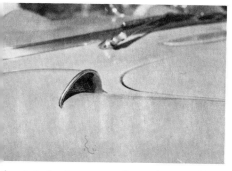

imulated air scoops have been added top the front fenders.

Tires are still 6:70 x 15, but blackwalls are standard now and these wide whitewall tires are an optional item. The new full wheel covers are standard equipment.

Among the color choices were several in which the side panels are painted a contrasting color.

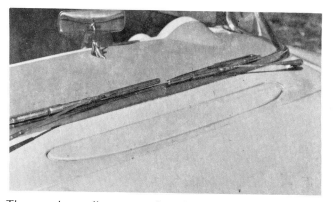

The cowl ventilator remains, but windshield washers have become an optional accessory.

1956

New this year is an attractive removable hard top. The Corvette was offered with either hard or soft-top as standard, or optionally, with both.

The fuel tank is still located behind the seats and filled through a filler tube under a lid on the left rear fender.

Outside push-button door handles are added i 1956 and for the first time the car can be locke from the outside.

The view from the rear differs sharply from 1955 largely due to the elimination of the podded tail lights.

Placed on the rear deck above a convenient key lock is this newly designed ornament which is also used on the hood.

Dual Exhaust pipes exit through concentric rings formed in the rear bumpers.

Gone are the rear light "pods" of 1955, replaced by lights smoothly faired into the rear fenders.

The rear lamp lens is placed in a scoop-shaped chromed housing in the fender.

Rear deck appears to slope downwards more sharply than it actually does due to emphasis of the shape of the fenders.

Chromed bumper sections are used on each side of a centrally placed license plate holder.

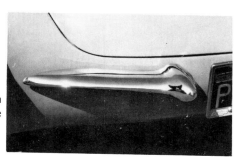

Fenders are protected with bumpers curved above and also below center line.

Roll-up windows were introduced on the 1956 Corvette. Due to the geometry of the opening though, it was necessary for them to appear to rotate slightly as they lowered. Chromed trim surrounds the window well at the top of the door (below).

A removable hard top was offered by the factory as an alternate to the folding soft top. For the first time, Corvette became a truly enclosed car with the additional comfort. An option offered allowed purchasers to obtain both tops with their car. Another option offered a power mechanism for folding the soft top.

When introduced, the hard tops lacked this trim strip. Shortly afterward, having discovered a paint separation problem at the forward edge, a trim strip was added.

Chromed latches, installed in the tops secure them to hooks placed at the top of the windshield.

The interior of the removable hard top is upholstered with a waffle pattern material matching the inserts of the seats.

The soft top latching brackets are chromed and have integral studs which protrude through the deck and are then locked with a nut beneath.

The attractive rear quarter window is actually a part of the removable hard top. It cannot be lowered.

A wide rear window is provided having no interrupting dividers. The two latches which appear on the deck are used for anchoring the back edge of the soft top and are not used with the hard top.

A new rotary latch has been provided in the luggage compartment.

Rear deck lid opens to reveal luggage compartment. The spare wheel is stored under the deck of this compartment.

Part number of the 1956 rubber mat differs from that on the 1954 (page 38).

The design of the new rotary trunk latch require a greater clearance of the rubber trunk mat which while similar in appearance, is not identical wit that in the earlier car.

Since glass windows now recess into the doors, the storage pockets found there formerly are now eliminated. For comfort, a protruding arm rest has been added in their place.

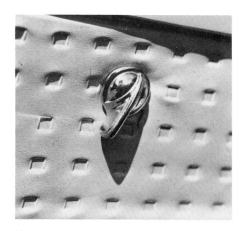

New this year is the inside door lock and chromed knob.

In addition to the standard wind-up windows, an option this year, for the first time, adds the convenience of power-operated windows.

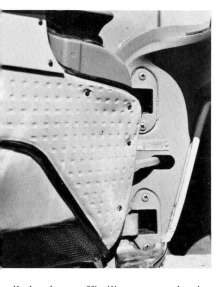

The familiar white knob on inside door release lever is unchanged.

distinctive waffle-like pattern in the interior upholstery is carried over onto the door. The serial number plate has been moved from the cowl (page 42) to the door frame.

1956

The waffle-patterned upholstery, new this year, will again appear in the 1957 Corvette.

Still a two-passenger vehicle, the 1956 Corvette employed a different pattern on its seats than the 1955 model. Bolsters are narrower, seat and back portion wider this year.

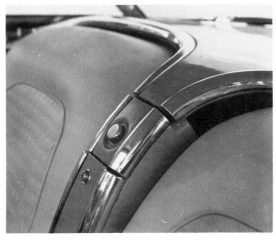

Having eliminated the storage compartments in the doors, a new location was found for a compartment between the seats and below the release knob for the lid of the top storage compartment.

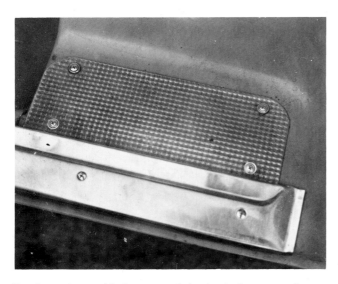

Set into the molded recess of the body is a step plate, but its location is more decorative than practical.

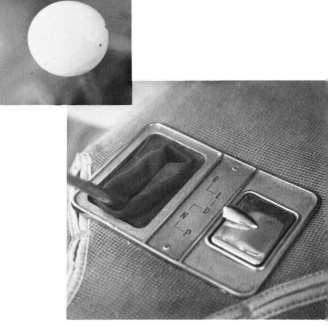

Although Powerglide automatic transmission continued to be available, it was an optional accessory. Standard for the 1956 Corvette is a 3-speed manual transmission.

nstruments continue to be balanced around the achometer set in the center of the instrument panel.

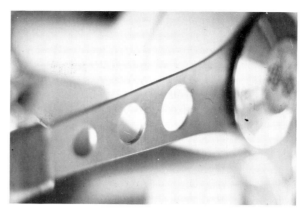

A new competition type steering wheel for 1956 has three flat steel spokes.

The new three-spoked steering wheels are available in both red and in beige.

Imprinted in the center of the horn button in the Corvette name.

e defroster outlet vent on the top surface the instrument panel (seen through the ndshield) resembles the same unit used in e previous model, but is actually somewhat orter.

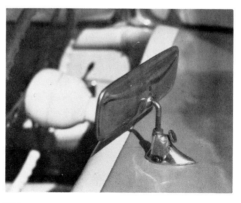

This adjustable-height inside rear view mirror is unique to 1956 only.

1956

The 140 mph speedometer is clear and visible.

New knobs appear on the instrument panel controls.

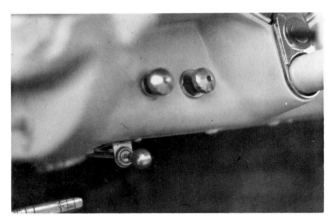

The hood release is suspended under the instrument panel to the right of the parking brake release handle and has a chromed knob.

Although the instrument panel layout appears unchanged, the 1956 ignition lock has a new escutcheon plate (page 63).

For 1956 the cowl ventilator control handle has been fitted with a chromed knob in place of the earlier plastic one.

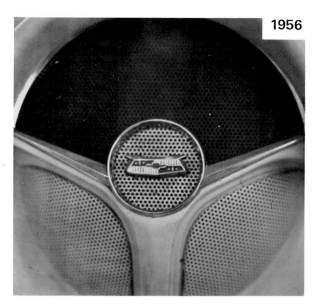

arger, disc-shaped knobs are used on the 1956 strument panel. To the right of the radio tuning ob is a cigarette lighter.

The radio speaker again is housed behind this grill at the right side of the instrument panel.

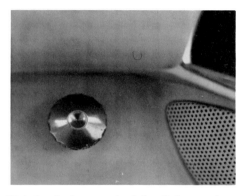

This knob, just to the left of the speaker grill operates the heater blower motor.

A new radio is introduced in 1956. Still a Wonder-bar tuning unit, it has been sharply restyled and is again used in 1957. Radio is an extra cost option, as is heater.

The instruments are unchanged in form or location.

n escutcheon plate has been lded and the ignition lock no nger is serrated (page 63).

This 6000 rpm tachometer was introduced with the V-8 engines in the 1955 model.

CHEVROLET'S NEW CORVETTE

FUN!

"Every Inch a Champion"

Six solid colors and six two-tones are offered for 1957. They are: black, copper, white, green, blue, and red in solid; and black & silver, copper & beige, white & silver, green & beige, blue & silver, and red & beige.

SPECIFICATIONS

ENGINE

Valve-in-head V8, 283-cubic-inch displacement, 3.88" bore x 3.0" stroke, 9.5 to 1 compression ratio. 220 h.p. at 4800 r.p.m. with 4-barrel carburetor. 245 h.p. at 5000 r.p.m. with twin 4-barrel carburetion.* 250 h.p. at 5000 r.p.m. with Ramjet Fuel Injection system.* High-lift camshaft, hydraulic valve lifters. Independent operating mechanism for each valve. Cast aluminum rocker covers on optional engines. Buffed aluminum racing-type oil-wetted air cleaners, chrome plated single air cleaner with fuel injection. Five-bearing forged steel crankshaft. Special replaceable-insert main and connecting rod bearings. Full-pressure lubrication system with full-flow oil filter. Full dual exhaust system. Shielded ignition, 12-volt electrical system. Engine precision balanced after assembly.
Maximum performance 283 h.p. at 6200 r.p.m. engine* available only with close-ratio Synchro-Mesh features Ramjet Fuel Injection system, 10.5 to 1 compression ratio, competition-type camshaft, and high-speed valve system with special valve springs, spring dampers, and mechanical valve lifters.

TRANSMISSION

Choice of special 3-speed close-ratio Synchro-Mesh (2.2:1 low and reverse, 1.31:1 second, 1:1 high) with high-capacity 10-inch semi-centrifugal coil spring clutch, or optional Powerglide special automatic transmission.* Floor-mounted gear or range selector.

CHASSIS

Drive System—Hotchkiss drive, with unit-balanced tubular propeller shaft and universal joints.
Rear Axle—Semi-floating hypoid with single unit banjo housing. Axle ratios: with Powerglide, 3.55:1; with close-ratio Synchro-Mesh 3.70:1. Positraction axle with 3.70:1, 4.11:1, or 4.56:1 ratio optional* with close-ratio Synchro-Mesh only.
Frame—Extra-rigid box girder frame reinforced with "X" member.
Suspension—Independent coil spring front suspension with ride stabilizer. Outrigger mounted semi-elliptic rear springs. Direct double-acting shock absorbers.
Steering—Full anti-friction steering gear with balanced steering linkage, 16:1 overall ratio. Turning diameter (curb to curb), 36.55 feet right, 36.93 feet left.

Brakes—Hydraulic 11-inch self-energizing brakes with bonded linings. Mechanical parking brake on rear wheels.
Wheels and Tires—Choice of black or white sidewall* 6.70-15 4-ply tubeless tires. Chrome wheel covers with simulated knock-off hubs.
Fuel Tank—16.4-gallon capacity. Filler cap concealed in left fender.

EXTERIOR FEATURES

Glass-fibre-reinforced plastic body with sculptured side panels. High quality polished lacquer finish. Front hinged hood with inside latch release and automatic support. Large luggage locker with spare wheel well under floor, concealed top well behind seats. Dual exhaust ports. Chrome-bound windshield. Large screened cowl ventilator. Manually operated fabric top or lightweight easily removable plastic hardtop. Power-operating mechanism optional* with fabric top.

INTERIOR FEATURES

Foam rubber padded, all-vinyl trimmed bucket seats, individually adjustable with safety belt* and shoulder harness.* Wide doors with built-in arm rest, pushbutton door handle, key lock, inside door release. Choice of crank-operated or power* window lifts. Ash tray and glove compartment between seats; simulated roll on instrument panel and doors, rubber-backed carpeting, metal door kick panels, sills, and step plates. Competition-type steering wheel with three spring steel spokes. Speedometer, tachometer, ammeter, fuel level, oil pressure, and coolant temperature gauges. Signal-seeking transistorized radio,* heater,* directional signals, electric clock, cigarette lighter, outside and inside rear-view mirror, dual electric windshield wipers, windshield washer.

COLORS

The 1957 Corvette is available in your choice of six solid exterior colors or six two-tone combinations with color-keyed interior and matching or contrasting top.

DIMENSIONS

Wheelbase, 102". Length, 168". Overall height: top down, 49.2"; convertible top, 51.1"; hardtop, 51". Height at door, 33". Road clearance, 5.8". Width, 70.5". Tread, 57" front, 59" rear.

*Optional at extra cost.

1957 saw the start of Corvette's drive for power and all engines became 283 cid. In addition to the standard 220 horsepower engine, an optional offering included a two-carburetor set up rated at 245 hp, and a new fuel injected 250 hp engine. Having gone this far, Chevrolet offered yet another all-out optional engine with mechanical lifters, 10.5:1 compression, tuned valve system and fuel injection. This maximum-performance engine poured out a heavy 283 hp at 6200 rpm.

Introduced with Chevrolet's 3-speed standard transmission, and Powerglide automatic available as an option, later in the year an all-new 4-speed transmission was made available and went on to become a most popular option.

Appearance changes are minimal, limited to the addition of side insignia on the cars having other than the standard "small" engine.

1957 Corvette

Mr. Bob Wingate, Glendora, California

This emblem is also used on the rear deck.

The massive appearance of the front end is unchanged from 1956.

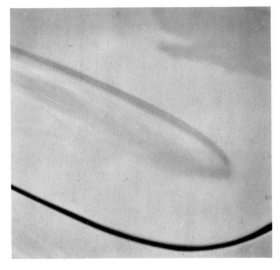

This is the last year for this hood panel with its two longitudinal raised sections. Introduced on the first model, the hood has been interchangable until now.

1957 is the last year for this heavy-looking 13-tooth wide grill.

The non-functional decorative fender scoops will be eliminated in 1958.

1957 is the last year of this single-lamp headlight arrangement.

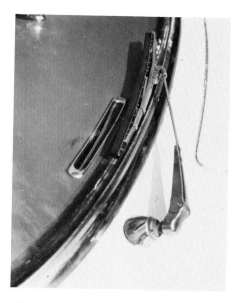

Dual electric windshield wipers are standard, but a washer is optional.

Standard for the car is 6:70 x 15 blackwall tires, but whitewalls are offered as options. Wheel covers are unchanged from 1956 and are standard for the car.

Choice of one of the two new fuel injected engines called for the inclusion of the nameplate on the side panels of the front fenders.

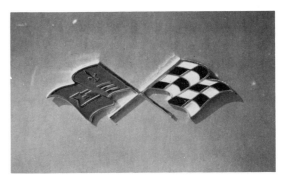

These crossed flags appear on the sides of the 1957 Corvettes equipped with fuel injection.

In addition to having the identification on the fenders, the 1957 fuel injection engined cars also carried the plate on the rear deck.

The 1957 Corvette equipped with the standard 220 hp engine was furnished with the fender panels bare like all of the 1956 models.

The dual exhaust pipes continue to exit through the tips of the bumpers.

Tail lights are unchanged from 1956 style.

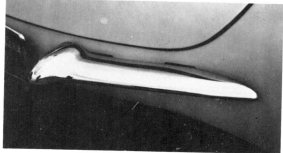

Again, chromed bumper center sections provide pleasant appearance as well as protection.

This antenna, mounted on the rear fender, was introduced in 1956 and replaces the former molded-in antenna in the rear deck lid.

A well, under the deck of the luggage compartment, accommodates the spare wheel.

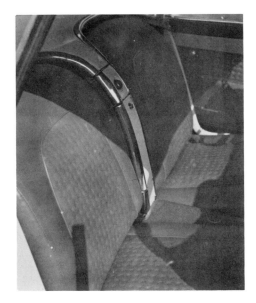

Interiors are again upholstered in the waffle-patterned vinyls used in 1956. Safety belts, first available in 1956 as options, are joined by optional shoulder harnesses.

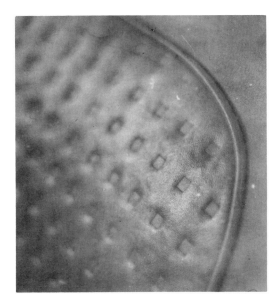

Seats are nicely trimmed with a piping to hide the seam.

Cars not having the optional power windows (page 79), are supplied with a window riser (below right). The location is more forward on the door and lower, a more convenient position for cranking.

Rotary, rather than latching, door locks have been used since the start.

The manual window crank handle is chromed.

Both beige, and also red, steering wheels were furnished with the steering column painted to match.

A new mirror, with a simplified base, is used in 1957.

...asically the same as the 1956 instrument panel, 1957 continues the ...e of a padded roll at the top of the panel.

The cowl ventilator is opened with this handle.

The 140 mph speedometer is unchanged.

A parking brake warning light continues to be furnished as an option.

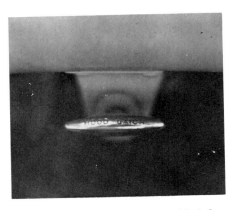

A new T handle is now provided for the hood latch.

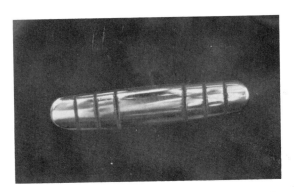

The parking brake handle continues unchanged and is again used to mechanically apply the rear wheel brakes.

During 1957 a new 4-speed competition style mission became available as an option. In additi the standard three-speed and another option, P glide automatic, this gave the buyer his choice three transmissions and four engines.

A new inside rear view mirror in 1957 eliminates the screw adjustment found on the 1956 style (page 81).

Radios are generally considered optional accessories, but are almost invariably purchased with the car. For occasions when they are not, suitable blanking plates are available.

In addition to a safe operating greenline, a new 7000 rpm tachometer is provided with a red line commencing at the appropriate spot depending upon the engine.

The escutcheon plate that had been added to the 1956 ignition lock is now eliminated although the appearance of the lock itself is unchanged.

Ramjet Fuel Injection unit is this manifold assembly located atop the block between the valve chambers. Unit at the top is incoming air filter, below the manifold is the fuel metering assembly.

This is the control device that determines the amount of fuel to be passed through the manifold into the cylinders. It performs this function by adjusting a butterfly valve in the incoming filtered air line.

A fuel filter is mounted just ahead of the right-side valve chamber.

In addition to providing a dual-carburetor version of their new 283 engine, in 1957, Chevrolet offered a further inducement—fuel injection.

Basically, fuel injection is a constant flow fuel system that delivers fuel directly to the cylinders eliminating the carburetor. With some additional changes, including a high compression (10.5:1) ratio, special camshaft, special valve springs, and mechanical lifters, a senior version of Corvette's new 283 cubic inch engine was offered with a rating of 283 horsepower, or a never-before-heard-of one horsepower per cubic inch of displacement.

The nine-ribbed cast aluminum valve covers are used on the 1957 injected engines only. Later covers have only seven ribs.

Fuel Injection remained a Corvette option from its introduction on the 1957 model until it was replaced in mid-1965
with the big block Turbo-Jet 396 engine.

Similar in appearance to the standard shielding, this one, for
use with fuel injection, differs and the two do not interchange.

In addition to the serial number, the Fuel Injection nameplate
also bears a model number. These apply as follows:

YEAR	HORSEPOWER	MODEL NUMBER
1957	250 or 283	7014360 or 7014520
1958	250	7014900
1958	290	7014900R or 7014960
1959	250	7014900
1959	290	7014900-R, 7017250, or 7017300
1960-61	275	7017310
1960-61	315	7017320
1962	360	7017355 or 7017360
1963	360	7017375
1964	375	7017375-R or 7017380
1965	375	7017380

Each fuel injection unit is provided with a nameplate
indicating its serial number which bears no relation to
that of the car. All fuel injection units were manufactured by Rochester, a supplier.

"SWEETEST TWO-SEATER GOING"

SPECIFICATIONS

ENGINE: Valve-in-head V8, 283-cubic-inch displacement, 3.88" bore x 3.0" stroke, 9.5:1 compression ratio. 230 H.p. with 4-barrel carburetor. 245 h.p. with twin 4-barrel carburetion*. 250 h.p. with Ramjet Fuel Injection*. High-lift camshaft, hydraulic valve lifters. Independent operating mechanism for each valve. Precision-machined forged steel crankshaft, five main bearings. Special alloy main and connecting rod bearings. Full-pressure lubrication system with full-flow oil filter. 12-volt electrical system. Engine precision-balanced after assembly. Finned aluminum rocker covers on optional engines. Buffed aluminum oil-wetted air cleaner (paper-element type with fuel injection). Full dual exhaust system. Maximum performance 290 h.p. engine* features Ramjet Fuel Injection, 10.5:1 compression ratio, special camshaft, and high-speed valve system with special valves and mechanical valve lifters. **TRANSMISSION:** Special 3-speed close-ratio Synchro-Mesh (2.2:1 low and reverse, 1.31:1 second and 1:1 high) standard. Close-ratio 4-speed Synchro-Mesh* optional (2.2:1 first, 1.66:1 second, 1.31:1 third, 1:1 fourth, 2.25:1 reverse). 10" semi-centrifugal coil spring clutch. Powerglide automatic transmission* available with 230, 245, and 250 horsepower engines. Floor-mounted gear or range selector. **REAR AXLE:** Semi-floating hypoid. Axle ratios: 3-speed or 4-speed Synchro-Mesh 3.70:1; Powerglide 3.55:1. Positraction rear axle with choice of 3.70:1, 4.11:1, or 4.56:1 ratio optional* with either 3-speed or 4-speed Synchro-Mesh. **CHASSIS:** Box-girder, X-member reinforced frame. Independent coil spring front suspension with stabilizer bar. Outrigger-mounted semi-elliptic rear springs. Direct double-acting shock absorbers. Unit-balanced tubular propeller shaft and universal joints. Full anti-friction steering gear and balanced linkage—21:1 overall ratio. Hydraulic 11-inch self-energizing brakes, with fade-resistant linings. Mechanical parking brake on rear wheels. 16.4 gallon fuel tank. Black 6.70 x 15 4-ply rating tubeless tires, wh sidewall tires optional*. Chrome wheel covers with simulated knock-off hu **EXTERIOR:** Glass-fiber-reinforced plastic body—sculptured side panels. Polish acrylic lacquer finish. Front hinged hood. Three-unit front grille. Dual headlig in front fenders. Cowl ventilator. Large luggage locker with spare wheel und floor. Concealed well for folding top behind seats. Chrome-bound windshie Functional, wraparound front and rear bumpers mounted to the frame. D exhaust ports in rear bumpers. Choice of manually operated fabric folding t or easily removable plastic hardtop. **INTERIOR:** Foam rubber padded, c vinyl trimmed bucket seats, individually adjustable. Safety belts. Pushbut door handles, key lock, inside release. Long padded armrest on each doo Crank-operated windows. Vinyl covered instrument panel crown and doo Passenger assist bar in instrument panel cove. Carpeted floor, metal d scuff panels, sills and step plates. Competition-type steering wheel. Spee ometer, tachometer, ammeter, fuel level, oil pressure, and coolant tempe ture gauges, starter-ignition switch, and light switch on instrument pan Directional signals, cigarette lighter, outside and inside rearview mirro dual electric windshield wipers, electric clock. Ashtray and glove compa ment between seats. **OPTIONAL*:** Engines, transmissions, axle, and wh sidewall tires (see above). Power-operating mechanism and removable plas hardtop with folding top. Power windows. Transistorized radio, heat windshield washer. Heavy-duty brakes-and-suspension package. Special whee **DIMENSIONS:** Wheelbase, 102". Length, 177.2". Overall height: folding to 51.1" up, 49.2" down; hardtop, 51". Height at door, 33". Road clearanc 5.8". Width, 72.8". Tread: 57" front, 59" rear.

*Optional at extra co

1958 brought an obvious change in Corvette's appearance. New, dual headlights appeared at the front fenders along with a revised grill both of which added to the appearance. Styling had a field day with addition of dummy louvers on the hood and chromed trim lines on the trunk. With three transmissions to chose from (three-speed was standard), buyers also could ponder their choice of four engines from the standard 230 hp all the way up to a new "maximum performance" 290 hp featuring not only fuel injection, but also a special valve train using mechanical lifters. A further choice of three rear axle ratios with a new limited slip differential called Positraction completed the range.

With variations featuring maximum performance as well as the latest in styling, Corvette had become not only a sports car but also a fine leisure car and, for the year, Chevrolet was moved to call it the . . . "Sweetest Two-Seater Going!".

1958

A distinguishing feature of the 1958 Corvette is this louvered hood panel.

1958 Corvette

Mrs. Deo Holmquist, Lemon Grove, California

Another distinguishing feature is the two chromed bars on the rear deck.

1958

A new, narrower, 9 tooth grill adds to the apparent width of the car.

A revision of the front emblem which continues to resemble the earlier style, presents the name in bold letters rather than script.

Dual headlamps are introduced, and with them, a styling feature in which a graceful trim strip divides the fender almost to the windshield.

Wheelcover is unchanged from the style introduced in 1956. 6:70 x 15 blackwall are standard, whitewalls an option.

A grill-work of 18 non-functional louvers has been added to the hood. However, serving no purpose other than decorative, they were deleted the following year.

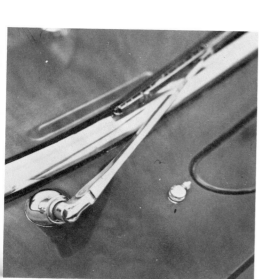

Dual electric windshield washers are continued as standard as is the cowl ventilator, but the windshield washers are an optional accessory.

Chromed bezels surround the new twin-lamp headlights.

Parking lights are well recessed for better protection.

Decorative air scoops appear at the ends of the grill but do not open and serve no useful purpose.

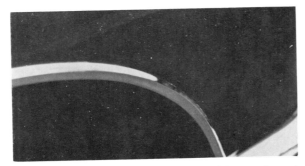

A chromed trim strip outlines the side panels and decorates the edge of the wheel housing.

The new massive front bumper sweeps cleanly arou the fender, adding to the over-all sturdy appearan of the front end.

Corvette's crossed flag insignia is continued on the fenders.

Adding to the effect of the "scoop" at the ends of the front grill are "exhausts" placed in the side panels.

The 1958 rear deck is decorated by two heavy chromed strips, and is the only year in which these were employed.

The curve of the top of the rear fender harmonizes with the radiused wheel well.

The 1958 Owners Manual describes the Corvette's antenna installation on the *right* rear fender, and this Dealer-installed antenna is so placed. However, factory-installed antenna installations continued to be placed on the *left* rear fender, thus ignoring the Company's own literature.

Outside door handles and key lock are continued unchanged.

A new tail light housing and lens retains the attractive curved lines of the fender, but encloses the light (see page 74) in a more attractive manner. A narrow trim strip serves to emphasize the crown of the fender.

New massive rear bumpers wrap cleanly around the rear fenders.

The massive look of the front end has been repeated with a new treatment of the rear. Bumpers have been made heavier, and a pair of curiously shaped trim pieces (right) applied on the deck.

Reflectors have been placed on the rear fenders below the tail lights. Manufactured by the Guide Division, their name is molded in.

A keylock is continued in place on the rear deck.

The dual exhausts exit through the bumpers.

New license plate lights are built into the inner ends of the bumpers.

Buyers got their choice; either a folding soft top, *or* a plastic hard top, or both. Since the soft top was not as attractive as the hardtop with its excellent lines, the hard top was a popular choice.

The wide chrome trim band at the forwa edge of the hard top flows gracefully into t windshield frame.

The windows in the hardtops are not glass, but plexiglas, and they are susceptible to scratching. However, the use of plastic served to substantially reduce the weight of the tops.

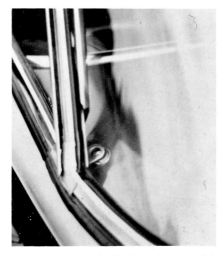

The hard top is locked to the car with latches at the windshield frame and with two bolts which are placed through holes in side brackets, and threaded into sockets set in the body.

The interior of the hard top is upholstered in a wide-striped vinyl reminiscent of the trunk matting.

hese latches are used to
nchor the soft top only.

To raise the soft top, the hard
top must be removed and this
lid behind the seats raised.

The latching brackets on the rear deck
have been revised (page 77), and are
now fastened to the deck with nuts
and bolts.

Soft tops are not re-
moved from the car,
but are folded into this
storage well.

nlike the removable hard top, the
oft top has no quarter windows and
he opening is tailored to fit the
ntegral window.

Although a power-operated erection mechanism was an available option, most tops
were furnished without that accessory.

In erecting the soft top, the storage compartment is opened (preceeding page), and the folded assembly withdrawn (bottom photo). Unfolding the metal bow assembly stretches the front bow forward where it may be secured with the clamping latches to the windshield frame. Next the rear bow is unfolded to the deck and latched (top photo).

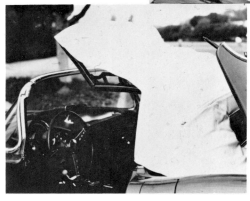

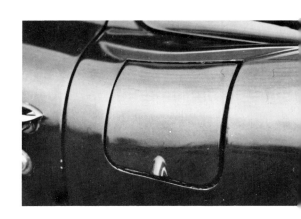

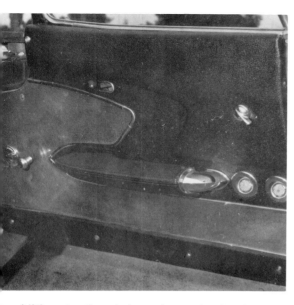

In addition to the obvious change in the flowing lines of the trim, the arm rest has become a separate and distinct item.

The unchanged inside door lock remains, on a background of distinctive pebble-grained vinyl upholstery.

In place of the waffle pattern of 1957, a new attractive metal trim appears behind the window riser.

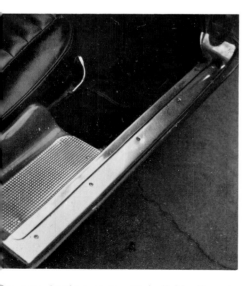

The two bucket seats are individually adjustable. This handle releases the latch on the passenger's seat.

Dual safety reflectors now appear on the bottom of the doors to warn oncoming traffic when the doors are opened.

1958

A new dashboard layout appears in 1958. This is a photograph taken in 1957.

Below the push-button release for the top storage well cover is a locking push-button for the glove compartment.

This passenger assist bar is new this year. The radio speaker formerly found in this location has been moved to the top center suface area of the instrument panel.

The exterior colors available for 1958 include Signet Red, Panama Yellow, Regal Turquois, Silver Blue, Snowcrest White, Charcoal and Inca Silver.

The colors used in the interiors were Signet Red, Charcoal, and Silver Blue.

The competition type three-spoke steering wheel is unchanged from the style introduced in 1956. Steering wheels were selected to match the instrument panel color.

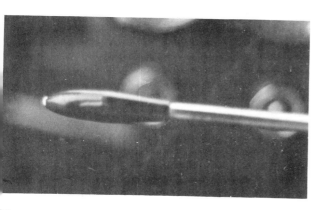

The turn signal lever matches the color of the steering wheel.

A new speedometer with a maximum reading of 160 rather than the earli 140 mph is an indication of the times. With their maximum performan engine options, buyers might have made it, but the ordinary standa performance cars at least could enjoy the suggestion of the need for higher upper limit.

The standard tachometer reads to 60 (6000 rpm), but the maximum performance engine, capable of that and more, was furnished with a special tach- omer reading up to 8000 rpm.

Two radios were offered in Corvette in 1958 (and 1959). This is the transistorized Push Button radio, a less costly option that the other radio, a Wonder Bar signal-seeking set.

The top surface of the instrument panel is upholstered in the pebble-grain vinyl as is the roll at the bottom.

A new center console houses the radio, heater controls, and clock.

An electric clock is a standard item in Corvette not an accessory.

Chevrolet **CORVETTE**

AMERICA'S SPORTS CAR

SPECIFICATIONS

FOR PERFORMANCE

CORVETTE ENGINES are 283-cubic-inch displacement valve-in-head V8's with 3.88″ bore and 3.0″ stroke.

230-H.P. CORVETTE V8 with 4-barrel carburetion, 9.5:1 compression ratio, hydraulic valve lifters, standard equipment.

245-H.P. CORVETTE V8* with twin 4-barrel carburetion, 9.5:1 compression ratio, hydraulic valve lifters.

250-H.P. CORVETTE V8* with Ramjet Fuel Injection, 9.5:1 compression ratio, hydraulic valve lifters.

270-H.P. CORVETTE V8* with twin 4-barrel carburetion, 9.5:1 compression ratio, special camshaft and high-speed valve system with special valves and mechanical valve lifters.

290-H.P. CORVETTE V8* with Ramjet Fuel Injection, 10.5:1 compression ratio, special camshaft and high-speed valve system with special valves and mechanical valve lifters.

All engines have independent operating mechanism for each valve. Precision-machined forged steel crankshaft, five main bearings. Full pressure lubrication system with full-flow oil filter. 12-volt electrical system. Engines precision balanced after assembly. Finned aluminum rocker covers on optional engines. Buffed aluminum oil-wetted type air cleaner (special paper element, tube intake type with Fuel Injection). Full dual exhaust system.

CHOICE OF TRANSMISSIONS

3-SPEED CLOSE-RATIO SYNCHRO-MESH, standard equipment. Ratios: 2.21:1 low; 1.32:1 second; 1:1 third; 2.51:1 reverse. Floor mounted gearshift.

4-SPEED CLOSE-RATIO SYNCHRO-MESH.* Ratios: 2.2:1 first; 1.66:1 second; 1.31:1 third; 1.1 fourth; 2.26:1 reverse with manually operated mechanism on floor mounted shift lever to prevent unintentional reverse engagement during shifting.

POWERGLIDE* AUTOMATIC available with 230-, 245- and 250-horsepower engines. Floor mounted range selector lever.

CLUTCH. 10″ semi-centrifugal coil spring.

POWER-MATCHED REAR AXLES

Semi-floating hypoid.

STANDARD REAR AXLE RATIOS: 3.70:1 with 3-Speed or 4-Speed Synchro-Mesh; 3.55:1 with Powerglide.

POSITRACTION* REAR AXLE RATIOS: choice of 3.70:1, 4.11:1, or 4.56:1 ratio with either 3-Speed or 4-Speed Synchro-Mesh.

CHASSIS

Box-girder, X-member reinforced frame. Independent coil spring front suspension with stabilizer bar. Rear suspension by radius rods and outrigger-mounted semi-elliptic leaf springs. Direct double-acting shock absorbers. Unit-balanced tubular propeller shaft and universal joints. Full anti-friction steering gear and balanced linkage—21:1 overall ratio. Hydraulic 11-inch self-energizing brakes with fade-resistant, bonded linings, heavy-duty sintered-metallic brake linings optional*. Mechanical parking brake on rear wheels. 16.4-gallon fuel tank. Black 6.70 x 15 4-ply rating Tyrex cord tubeless tires, white sidewall tires optional*. Vented chrome wheel covers with simulated knock-off hubs.

SPECIAL EQUIPMENT* FOR SPORTS CAR MEETS

Heavy-duty front and rear springs and larger shock absorbers with stiffer valving, heavier front stabilizer and fast steering linkage that gives a 16.3:1 overall ratio. Special brakes with ceramic-metallic facings, finned cast iron brake drums and vented flange plates with air scoops. Used with Positraction rear axle, this equipment is available with 3-Speed or 4-Speed Synchro-Mesh and 270- or 290-h.p. engines. Wide-base wheels with 5½″ rims available. Also nylon cord tires available.

BODY EXTERIOR

Fiber-glass reinforced plastic body—sculptured side panels. Magic-Mirror acrylic lacquer finish in seven solid colors: Tuxedo Black, Classic Cream, Frost Blue, Crown Sapphire, Roman Red, Snowcrest White, Inca Silver. These colors also available in optional* two-tone exteriors with color-keyed Inca Silver or Snowcrest White in the sculptured side panels. Front hinged hood. Three-unit front grille. Dual headlights in front fenders. Pushbutton door handles with key lock. Cowl ventilator. Large luggage locker with spare wheel under floor. Concealed well for folding top behind seats. Folding top available in white, black, turquoise or blue. Chrome-bound windshield. Frame-mounted front and rear bumpers. Dual exhaust ports in rear bumpers. Choice of manually operated rubberized cotton fabric folding soft top or easily removable plastic hardtop. If both tops are desired, the other is an extra-cost option. Power-operated mechanism* for folding soft top also available.

INTERIOR FEATURES

Interior colors in black, blue, red or turquoise keyed to exterior colors. Foam rubber padded, all-vinyl trimmed bucket seats, individually adjustable. Safety belts. Long padded armrest on each door. Recessed safety reflectors in door sidewall panels. Crank-operated windows, power-operated optional*. Vinyl-covered instrument panel crown and doors. Passenger assist bar in instrument panel cove. Stowage bin below passenger assist bar. Carpeted floor, metal door scuff panels, sills and step plates. Competition-type steering wheel. Speedometer, tachometer, ammeter, fuel level, oil pressure, and coolant temperature gauges, starter-ignition switch, and light switch on instrument panel. Directional signals, cigarette lighter, outside and inside rearview mirrors, dual electric windshield wipers, electric clock. Ashtray and glove compartment with key lock located between seats. Transistorized radio*, heater*, parking brake alarm*, courtesy light*, right and left-hand sunshades*, and pushbutton windshield washer* also available.

DIMENSIONS

Wheelbase, 102″. Overall length, 177.2″. Overall height: Soft top up, 51.6″; top down, 49.7″; hardtop 51.5″. Height at door, 33.5″. Road clearance, 6.0″. Overall width, 72.8″. Tread: front, 57″; rear, 59″.

*Optional at extra cost.

116

The 1958 Corvette had been received with some reservation by those who complained that its appearance had been diluted with the addition of the several non-functional trim items. Chevrolet's answer was to delete the phoney hood louvers and remove the chrome trim strips from the rear deck, but the other items remained and the car was essentially unchanged. Enthusiasts had entered modified 1958 'Vettes at Sebring and Daytona after the factory withdrew from racing in 1957, and news of their exploits traveled far. Although they were ostensibly not involved in racing, Chevrolet was nevertheless not above trading on the charisma of such adventures and their 1959 model was introduced as having been "born and bred for sports car performance".

The louvers have been removed from the hood.

1959 Corvette

Mr. Jerry Chandler, San Diego, California

The rear deck lid no longer has trim strips.

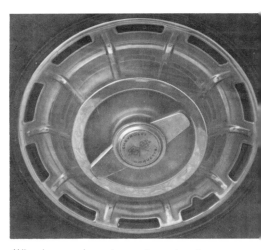

Wheelcovers have been slotted to increase cooling air flow at the brakes.

The 1959 hood now deletes the imitation louvers used on the 1958 car.

Aside from the obvious change in the hood, the 1959 front view differs little from that of 1958.

Both the inside and the outside rear view mirrors are standard equipment.

The two-tone effect in which the side panel is painted either Inca Silver or Snowcrest White is optional at extra cost.

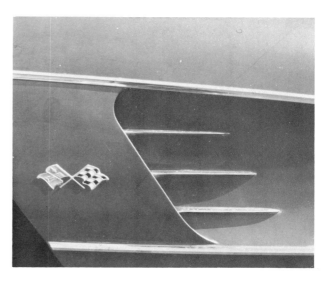

The recessed dummy vent is continued in 1959 as is the use of the crossed flags on the fender panel.

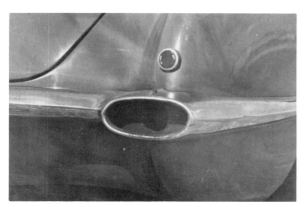

The two heavy chromed trim strips (page 107) used on the rear deck lid in 1958 have been omitted for 1959.

At the buyers choice, folding soft top, or this removable hard top were furnished. If *both* tops were ordered, one was an extra cost item.

The white plastic inside knob is unchanged, but the vinyl upholstery no longer is pebble-grained as in 1958.

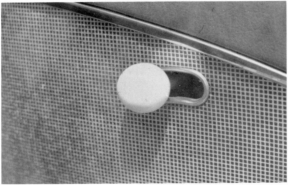

Hardly noticible, the inside door knob has been moved slightly forward from last year.

The competition type steering wheel is continued.

Manually operated windows a standard and as previously, power option is available at ext cost.

A new storage shelf has been added under the grab rail in front of the passenger's seat. Also new this year is a T-handle on the gear shift lever to prevent unintentional reverse shifting.

Seats have been re-shaped for added comfort. Still upholstered in vinyl over sponge rubber, the interiors are done in Red, Black, Turquoise Metallic or Light Blue Metallic.

A new 7000 rpm Tachometer is introduced which no longer includes a revolution totalizer as did the earlier units.

Mounted in the console is the Wonder Bar radio, one of two choices for 1958 and 59. The other radio is the Push Button model shown on page 115.

SPECIFICATIONS

FOR PERFORMANCE—CORVETTE ENGINES are 283-cubic-inch displacement valve-in-head V8's with 3.88" bore and 3.0" stroke • 230-H.P. CORVETTE V8 with 4-barrel carburetion, 9.5:1 compression ratio, hydraulic valve lifters, standard equipment. • 245-H.P. CORVETTE V8* with twin 4-barrel carburetion, 9.5:1 compression ratio, hydraulic valve lifters. • 275-H.P. CORVETTE V8* with Ramjet Fuel Injection, 11:1 compression ratio, aluminum cylinder heads, hydraulic valve lifters. • 270-H.P. CORVETTE V8* with twin 4-barrel carburetion, 9.5:1 compression ratio, special camshaft and high-speed valve system with special valves and mechanical valve lifters. All-aluminum cross-flow radiator included. • 315-H.P. CORVETTE V8* with Ramjet Fuel Injection, 11:1 compression ratio, aluminum cylinder heads, special camshaft and high-speed valve system with special valves and mechanical valve lifters. All-aluminum cross-flow radiator included.

All engines have independent operating mechanism for each valve. Precision-machined forged steel crankshaft, five main bearings. Full pressure lubrication system with full-flow oil filter. 12-volt electrical system. Engines precision balanced as assembly. Finned aluminum rocker covers on optional engines. Buffed aluminum oil-wetted type air cleaner (special paper element, tube intake type with Fuel Injection). Full dual exhaust system.

CHOICE OF TRANSMISSIONS—3-SPEED CLOSE-RATIO SYNCHRO-MESH, standard equipment. Ratios: 2.21:1 low; 1.32:1 second; 1:1 third; 2.51:1 reverse; floor mounted gearshift. 4-SPEED CLOSE-RATIO SYNCHRO-MESH.* (R.P.O. 685) Ratios: 2.2:1 first; 1.66:1 second; 1.31:1 third; 1.1 fourth; 2.26:1 reverse with manually operated mechanism on floor mounted shift lever to prevent unintentional reverse engagement during shifting. POWERGLIDE* AUTOMATIC (R.P.O. 313) available with 230- and 245-horsepower engines. Floor mounted range selector lever. CLUTCH. 10" semi-centrifugal coil spring.

POWER-MATCHED REAR AXLES—Semi-floating hypoid. STANDARD REAR AXLE RATIOS: 3.70:1 with 3-speed or 4-speed Synchro-Mesh; 3.55:1 with Powerglide. POSITRACTION* (R.P.O. 675) REAR AXLE RATIOS: choice of 3.70:1, 4.11:1 or 4.56:1 ratio with either 3-Speed or 4-Speed Synchro-Mesh.

CHASSIS—Box-girder, X-member reinforced frame. Independent coil spring front suspension with stabilizer bar. Rear suspension by radius rods and outrigger-mounted semi-elliptic leaf springs with stabilizer bar. Direct double action nitrogen bag shock absorbers. Unit-balanced tubular propeller shaft and universal joints. Full anti-friction steering gear and balanced linkage—21:1 overall ratio. Hydraulic 11-inch self-energizing brakes with fade-resistant, bonded linings. Mechanical parking brake on rear wheels.

16.4-gallon fuel tank. Black 6.70 x 15 4-ply rating Tyrex cord tubeless tires, wh sidewall tires optional*. Vented chrome wheel covers with simulated knock-off hu

SPECIAL EQUIPMENT* FOR SPORTS CAR MEETS—R.P.O. 687—Spe brakes with sintered-metallic facings, finned cast iron brake drums with buil cooling fan, vented flange plates with air scoops, and fast steering adapter for 16. overall ratio. Used with Positraction rear axle, this equipment is available with 3-Sp or 4-Speed Synchro-Mesh and 270- or 315-H.P. engine. R.P.O. 686—Special sinter metallic brake linings available with 3-Speed or 4-Speed Synchro-Mesh. F.O.A. 12 Temperature-controlled viscous drive fan. R.P.O. 276—Wide-base wheels with 5 rims. L.P.O. 1408—Nylon cord tubeless tires, 6.70 x 15 4-ply rating.

BODY EXTERIOR—Fiber-glass reinforced plastic body—sculptured side pan Magic-Mirror acrylic lacquer finish in eight solid colors: Tuxedo Black, Ermine Wh Roman Red, Sateen Silver, Horizon Blue, Tasco Turquoise, Cascade Green, Hondu Maroon. These colors also available in optional* two-tone exteriors with color-ke Sateen Silver or Ermine White in the sculptured side panels. Front hinged hood. Thr unit front grille. Dual headlights in front fenders. Pushbutton door handles and l lock. Cowl ventilator. Large luggage locker with spare wheel under floor. Concea well for folding top behind seats. Choice of manually operated rubberized fab folding soft top or easily removable plastic hardtop. Power-operating mechanis for folding soft top. Frame-mounted front and rear bumpers.

INTERIOR FEATURES—Interior colors in black, blue, red or turquoise keyed exterior colors. Foam rubber padded all-vinyl trimmed bucket seats, individu adjustable. Safety belts. Long padded armrest on each door. Recessed safety reflect in door sidewall panels. Crank-operated windows, power-operated optional*. Vin covered instrument panel. Passenger assist bar in instrument panel cove with stow bin below. Bright aluminum and vinyl sidewall trim. Carpeted floor, metal sills step plates. Competition-type steering wheel. Speedometer, tachometer, amme fuel level, oil pressure and coolant temperature gauges, starter-ignition switch, light switch on instrument panel. Directional signals, cigarette lighter, outside inside rearview mirrors, dual electric windshield wipers, electric clock. Ashtray glove compartment with key lock located between seats. Transistorized radio*, heate parking brake alarm*, courtesy light*, right- and left-hand sunshades*, and pu button windshield washer* also available.

DIMENSIONS—Wheelbase, 102". Overall length, 177.2". Overall height: Soft top 51.6"; top down, 49.7"; hardtop, 51.5". Height at door, 33.5". Road clearance, 5 Overall width, 72.8". Tread: front, 57"; rear, 59".   *Optional at extra c

fined still further, the 1960 Corvette offered buyers their choice from <u>five</u> engines ranging from the standard 230 *rsepower "small" engine all the way up to a 315 hp fuel injected version featuring a compression ratio of 11:1 and *minum heads. Three transmission options and three optional rear end ratios, Positraction Limited Slip Differential, *were there to seduce the speed fan. In addition though, Corvette offered niceties including optional power windows, *ite side wall tires, radio, heater, courtesy lights, and such standard features as fully carpeted floors, directional *nals, padded arm rests, and individually adjustable padded vinyl-covered bucket seats. Truly the car was . . . "de-*ned for personal sports car comfort".*

1960

1960 Corvette

Mr. Franz Eisele, Oceanside, California

In a futher effort to cool the brakes as much as possible, cars purchased with full competition options (including a stiffer suspension than was used on the stock version) were fitted with the standard Chevrolet small hub caps. Generally limited therefore to cars with the biggest of the engines, it was a surprise to find them on this one with "merely" a 270 hp twin-carburetor version. The car was re-fitted for this study with the standard wheel covers, but actually came equipped _originally_ with the hub caps shown in the photograph above.

This is the last year in which this distinctive emblem appears on the front hood.

From this angle there is no clue as to whether this is the 1960 model or last year's 1959.

The imposing "toothed" grill is last used in 19

The "scoops" at the front remain non-functional.

The chromed bezel, introduced on the 1958 model, is unchanged through 1960.

Identical with the 1959 hood, that of the 1960 has two longitudinal strengthening ribs.

The forward edge of the soft top, unlike that of the removable hard top, does not have a chrome trim.

This Guide Division mirror is correct from 1954 through 1962.

nder side of the front fen-
er well is trimmed with the
hrome trim that continues
o form the outline of the
ulptured side panel.

Again crossed flags appear on the fenders.

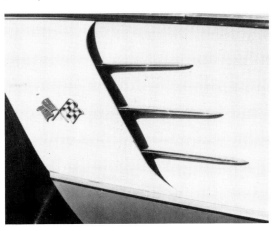

Again this year, the two-tone effect is an extra charge option.

Under the access cover on the left rear fender is a vented fuel filler cap.

1960 is the last year for this sloped rear deck.

First used in 1958, this emblem is continued on the rear deck lid through 1962.

The two reflectors at the rear are unchanged.

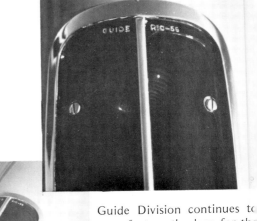

Guide Division continues to manufacture the lens for the rear fender lights.

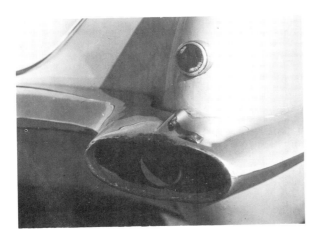

The sharply sloping rear deck is protected by a wrapped-around bumper.

The rear deck lid latch has been redesigned since its introduction in 1956 (page 78).

Although small, the luggage compartment will accommodate one or two ordinary suitcases.

As it did in 1959, the antenna appears on the *left* rear fender after one year of installation on the right in 1958.

Two of these attractive chromed handles latch the folding top to the windshield frame.

The snug-fitting folding soft top is available with a power-operated mechanism as an option. The plastic rear window is sewn in, not zippered.

On top of the doors, surrounding the window well, is a chromed frame.

The inside rear view mirror, mounted in the center, atop the instrument panel, is standard as is the outside rear view mirror. On the surface of the deck behind the mirror may be seen the grill over the radio speaker.

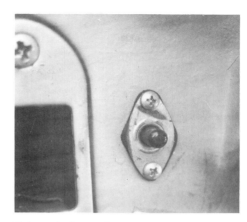

The trim on the doors has been changed to a highly reflective formed metal with a different pattern than was used in 1959 (page 122).

This switch on the door frame operates the courtesy lights when door is opened. The light is an option, not standard.

The door trim, which was embossed in 1959, (page 122) is now stitched for better effect.

The two reflectors introduced at the bottom of the doors in 1958 are continued.

Chromed caps are again provided at the rear of the arm rests on the doors.

The directional signal lever is white to match the other knobs.

In place of the horizontal seams of 1959, the 1960 interior has longitudinal seams on the seats. Interior colors for 1960 included Black, Red, Light Blue Metallic, and Turquoise Metallic.

A common owner-added accessory for the competition type steering wheel is this laced-on wheel cover.

he 160 mph speedometer is unchanged.

With the high performance 270 HP twin-carburetor engine that appears in this car, is furnished this 7000 rpm tachometer red-lined just above the point at which that rating is attained (6000 rpm).

The smaller instrument faces are flattened a bit but still seem to reflect the glare.

he T-shaped handle just be-
w the knob on the gear shift
as a welcome addition in
959 which prevented an in-
dvertent shift into reverse.

Again a storage compartment is provided below the indented instrument panel.

Again in 1960, the Wonder Bar radio is offered as an option, but unlike 1958 and 1959, the less costly Push Button radio option has been deleted.

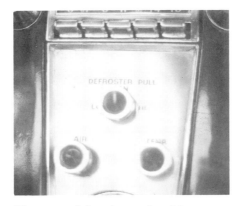

The control for the optional heater remain in the console just beneath the radio.

The electric clock, like the cigarette lighter, and ashtray has always been standard equipment and is not an extra.

This parking brake handle was first used 1958 replacing the earlier unlettered style 1957 (page 94).

The 1960 twin-carburetor performance engines (245 HP and 270 HP) were fitted with single large air cleaner for the two 4-barrel carburetors.

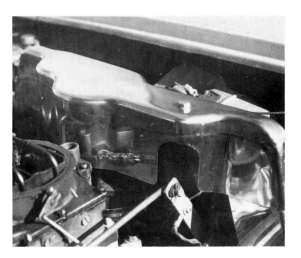

The distributor shielding is radiused to allow clearance for the accelerator push rod.

With cover and paper air filter removed, the base of the Air Cleaner assembly shows the intake areas of the two carburetors.

An adjustable mechanical linkage operates the two carburetors in parallel.

Cast aluminum covers are used on the valve chambers. These differ from similar covers used in 1958-59 (see page 308).

SPECIFICATIONS

ENGINE					TRANSMISSION	REAR AXLE	
H.P.	Induction System	Com-pression Ratio	Camshaft, Lifters	Distributor Points, Advance		Ratio	Positraction*
230 Std.	Single 4-Barrel	9.5:1	Regular, Hydraulic	Single, Vacuum & Centrifugal	3-Speed Synchro-Mesh 4-Speed Synchro-Mesh* Powerglide*	3.36:1 3.70:1 3.55:1	Yes Yes No
245*	Twin 4-Barrel	9.5:1	Regular, Hydraulic	Dual, Full Centrifugal	3-Speed Synchro-Mesh 4-Speed Synchro-Mesh* Powerglide*	3.36:1 3.70:1 3.55:1	Yes Yes No
270*	Twin 4-Barrel	9.5:1	Special, Mechanical	Dual, Full Centrifugal	3-Speed Synchro-Mesh 4-Speed Synchro-Mesh*	3.36:1 3.70:1	Yes Yes
275*	Ramjet Fuel Injection	11.0:1	Regular, Hydraulic	Single, Vacuum & Centrifugal	3-Speed Synchro-Mesh 4-Speed Synchro-Mesh*	3.36:1 3.70:1	Yes Yes
315*	Ramjet Fuel Injection	11.0:1	Special, Mechanical	Dual, Full Centrifugal	3-Speed Synchro-Mesh 4-Speed Synchro-Mesh*	3.36:1 3.70:1	Yes Yes

*Optional at extra cost.   **Choice of Positraction rear axle ratios: With 3-Speed Synchro-Mesh—3.36:1, 4.11:1, 4.56:1
With 4-Speed Synchro-Mesh—3.70:1, 4.11:1, 4.56:1

FOR PERFORMANCE. CORVETTE ENGINES are 283-cubic-inch displacement valve-in-head V8's with 3.88" bore and 3. stroke, precision balanced assembly. All engines have independent operating mechanism for each valve, precision-machine forged steel crankshaft, five main bearings, full-pressure lubrication system, full-flow oil filter, 12-volt electrical system, f dual exhaust. Oil-wetted, polyurethane element, buffed aluminum air cleaner (special paper element, tube intake wi Fuel injection). All-aluminum cross-flow radiator. Finned aluminum rocker covers on optional engines.
270*- and 315*-h.p. Corvette V8's feature special camshaft; high-speed valve system with special valves and mechanical val lifters; heavy-duty main and connecting rod bearings; distributor-driven tachometer; straight-through type mufflers. Fu Injection engines have special cylinder heads, pistons, and larger intake valves.

CHOICE OF TRANSMISSIONS. 3-SPEED SYNCHRO-MESH, standard equipment. Ratios: 2.47:1 low; 1.53:1 second; 1:1 high 2.80:1 reverse; floor-mounted gearshift. 4-SPEED CLOSE-RATIO SYNCHRO-MESH* (R.P.O. 685) Ratios: 2.2:1 first; 1.66 second; 1.31:1 third; 1.1 fourth; 2.26:1 reverse with manually operated mechanism on floor mounted shift lever to preve unintentional reverse engagement during shifting. CLUTCH, 10" semi-centrifugal coil spring. POWERGLIDE* AUTOMAT (R.P.O. 313) available with 230- and 245-horsepower engines. Floor mounted range selector lever.

POWER-MATCHED REAR AXLES. Semi-floating hypoid. Rear axle ratios matched to power team. Positraction (R.P.O. 67 rear axle optional* with 3- or 4-Speed Synchro-Mesh and choice of ratios (see chart above).

CHASSIS. Box-girder, X-member reinforced frame. Independent coil spring front suspension with stabilizer bar. Re suspension by radius rods and outrigger-mounted semi-elliptic leaf springs with stabilizer bar. Direct double-action nitroge bag shock absorbers. Unit-balanced tubular propeller shaft and universal joints. Full anti-friction steering gear and balance linkage—21:1 overall ratio. Hydraulic 11-inch self-energizing brakes with fade-resistant bonded linings. Hand-operated parki brake on rear wheels. 16.4-gallon fuel tank. Black 6.70 x 15 4-ply rating Tyrex cord tubeless tires, white sidewall tires optiona Vented chrome wheel covers with simulated knock-off hubs.

SPECIAL EQUIPMENT* FOR SPORTS CAR MEETS. R.P.O. 687—Special brakes with sintered-metallic facings, finne cast iron brake drums with built-in cooling fan, vented flange plates with air scoops, and fast steering adapter for 16.3:1 over ratio. Available with Positraction rear axle, 3-Speed or 4-Speed Synchro-Mesh, and 270- or 315-h.p. engine. R.P.O. 686—Speci sintered-metallic brake linings available with 3-Speed or 4-Speed Synchro-Mesh. F.O.A. 121—Temperature-controlled visco drive fan. R.P.O. 276—Wide-base wheels with 5½" rims; hub caps replace wheel covers. L.P.O. 1408—Nylon cord tubele tires, 6.70 x 15 4-ply rating. L.P.O. 1625A—24-gallon fuel tank.

BODY EXTERIOR. Fiber glass reinforced plastic body—sculptured side and rear panels. Magic-Mirror acrylic lacquer fini in seven solid colors: Tuxedo Black, Ermine White, Roman Red, Sateen Silver, Jewel Blue, Fawn Beige, Honduras Maroon. The colors also available in optional* two-tone exteriors with color-keyed Sateen Silver or Ermine White in the sculptured side pane Front hinged hood. Three-unit front grille. Dual headlights in front fenders. Four taillights. Push-button door handles and k lock. Cowl ventilator. Large luggage locker with spare wheel under floor. Concealed well for folding top behind seats. Choice manually operated rubberized fabric folding soft top or easily removable plastic hardtop. Power-operating mechanism* f folding soft top. Frame-mounted front and rear wraparound bumpers.

INTERIOR FEATURES. Interior colors in black, blue, red or fawn keyed to exterior colors. Foam rubber padded all-vin trimmed bucket seats, individually adjustable. Safety belts. Long padded armrest on each door. Recessed safety reflectors door sidewall panels. Crank-operated windows, power-operated optional*. Vinyl-covered padded instrument panel. Passeng assist bar in instrument panel cove with stowage bin below. Bright aluminum and vinyl sidewall trim. Carpeted floor, metal si and step plates. Competition-type steering wheel. Speedometer, tachometer, ammeter, fuel level, oil pressure and coola temperature gauges, starter-ignition switch with accessory position, and light switch on instrument panel. Directional signa cigarette lighter, outside and inside rearview mirrors, two-speed electric link-driven windshield wipers, electric clock. Parki brake alarm, courtesy light, right- and left-hand sunshades and push-button windshield washer. Ashtray and glove compartme with key lock located between seats. Transistorized push-button signal-seeking radio*, and heater* also available.

DIMENSIONS. Wheelbase, 102". Overall length, 177.7". Overall height: Soft top up, 52.2"; top down 50.2"; hardtop, 52. Height at door, 33.5". Road clearance, 6.7". Overall width, 70.4". Tread: front, 57"; rear, 59".

*optional at extra cost

1961 brought a change in the appearance of the front end with the abandoning of the traditional 9-tooth grill and the addition of the Corvette name on the hood. In the rear, additional luggage space was provided by redesigning the area for better effect. Other changes in the trim were more subtle such as the emblems on the fenders, and the addition of dual sun visors as standard equipment but on close inspection, it is true that for 1961, Corvette does meet the claim of the sales folder that . . . "America's Sports Car gets a New Look".

1961 Corvette

Midtown Motors, San Diego, California

1961

An entirely new frontal appearance is presented in the 1961 model Principal difference is the elimination of the traditional Corvette 11 tooth grill.

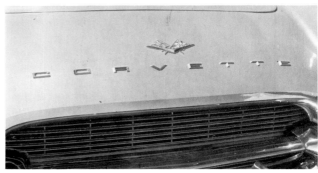

The name C-O-R-V-E-T-T-E is placed in block letters above the grill.

These crossed flags appear above the name. Gone is the round emblem of previous years.

The new rectangular-mesh grill is anodized to present bright finish. Across its center is a protective chrom bumper section.

e headlight rims are painted body color, a feature ich tends optically to extend the fenders. The ght chrome strip at the top of the fender remains.

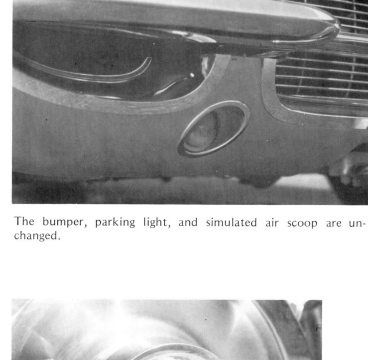

The bumper, parking light, and simulated air scoop are unchanged.

As in 1959, the wheel covers are slotted to permit more cooling air to be circulated around the brake drums. Tires are 6:70 x 15, and an option offers a special wide-base wheel with a 5½ inch rim on which hub caps (page 127) replace these standard wheel covers.

The three chromed spears departing from the simulated vents at the side are unchanged.

The flags, formerly found on the front fenders, have been replaced with this three-part trim insignia. The upper bar is red, the lower one blue. In the center is a bright strip bearing the name Corvette.

A new spring-loaded closing is provided for the fuel filler lid in place of the earlier style (page 129).

The rear end has been substantially redesigned to provide a larger storage area. In addition to the obvious changes in lights (below), the rear deck lid has been fitted with a central ridge which runs to the cockpit. This necessitates a modification of the tops to allow clearance for the strip. New bumpers omit the former concentric exhaust which now is located at the sides just ahead of the rear wheels.

Two rear lights (on each side) replace the previous fender-mounted tail lights.

The antenna is again mounted on the left rear fender.

The keylock for the rear deck has been relocated from the lid to a point on the body just above the rear license plate holder.

Following their custom of slightly altering the upholstery each year, the 1961 seats have a pattern similar to 1960 (page 134) but with a narrower pleat.

The competition type three-spoke steering wheel remains unchanged.

Interiors, color keyed to the outside paint, are furnished in black, blue, red, or fawn.

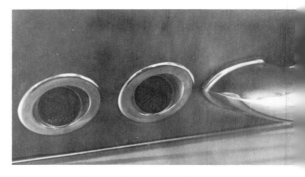

The two safety reflectors at the rear of the inside arm rests are unchanged.

The texture of the vinyl used on the door panels differs a bit from 1959.

The metal trim plate on the doors now is marked in a striped pattern in place of the 1959 "dotted" style (page 133).

This 7000 rpm tachometer, lacking a revolutions totalizing counter was introduced in 1960.

A new Wonder Bar radio was introduced in 1961, and offered again in 1962. As in the past, the radio continues to be an optional accessory at extra cost.

The electric clock is standard, but the heater-defroster is an option.

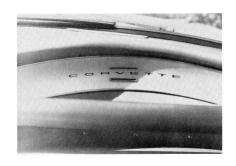

1962

"New Lines, New Leap, for America's Sports Car"

FOR 1962

SPECIFICATIONS

FOR PERFORMANCE—Corvette engines are 327-cubic-inch displacement valve-in-head V8s with 4.0" bore and 3.25" stroke, precision balanced as an assembly. All engines have in
pendent operating mechanism for each valve, precision-machined forged steel crankshaft, five premium aluminum main bearings, full-pressure lubrication system, full-flow oil filter, autom
choke, 12-volt electrical system, 30-amp. generator (35-amp. optional*), full dual exhaust. Oil-wetted, polyurethane element, buffed aluminum air cleaner (special tube intake type with
Injection). Distributor-driven tachometer. All-aluminum cross-flow radiator. Finned aluminum rocker covers and 35-amp. generator on high-output optional engines.
250-hp standard Corvette V8—Features 4-barrel carburetor, regular camshaft, hydraulic valve lifters, 10.5:1 compression ratio. Single point distributor, vacuum-centrifugal advance.
300-hp Corvette V8*—Features large aluminum-bodied 4-barrel carburetor, modified intake manifold, large intake valves, large exhaust manifolds, 10.5:1 compression ratio.
In addition, 340-hp (with large aluminum-bodied 4-barrel carburetor) and 360-hp (with Ramjet Fuel Injection) Corvette V8s* feature special cast iron cylinder heads with large p
domed aluminum pistons for 11.25:1 compression ratio and special camshaft; high-speed valve system with specially finished lightweight valves. Mechanical valve lifters. Dual p
distributor, full centrifugal advance.
CHOICE OF TRANSMISSIONS—3-SPEED SYNCHRO-MESH, standard equipment. Ratios: 2.47:1 low; 1.53:1 second; 1:1 third; 2.80:1 reverse; floor-mounted gearshift. 4-SPEED CLC
RATIO SYNCHRO-MESH*. RPO 685A (with standard 250- or optional 300-hp V8)—Ratios: 2.54:1 first; 1.92:1 second; 1.51:1 third; 1:1 fourth; 2.61:1 reverse. RPO 685B (with optional
or 360-hp V8)—Ratios: 2.20:1 first; 1.66:1 second; 1.31:1 third; 1:1 fourth; 2.26:1 reverse. Both 4-Speed transmissions have manually operated mechanism on floor mounted shift l
to prevent unintentional reverse engagement during shifting. CLUTCH: 10" semi-centrifugal coil spring. POWERGLIDE* AUTOMATIC (RPO 313 available with 250- and 300-hp Corvette
Floor mounted range selector lever.
POWER-MATCHED REAR AXLES—Semi-floating hypoid. Ratios matched to power team. Positraction (RPO 675) rear axle optional* with all transmissions. See power team chart for ra
CHASSIS—Box-Girder X-member reinforced frame. Independent coil spring front suspension with heavy stabilizer bar. Rear suspension by radius rods and outrigger-mounted semi-elli
leaf springs with stabilizer bar. Direct double-action nitrogen bag shock absorbers. Unit-balanced tubular propeller shaft and universal joints. Full anti-friction steering gear and balar
linkage—21:1 overall ratio. Hydraulic 11-inch self-energizing brakes with fade-resistant bonded linings. Hand-operated parking brake on rear wheels. 16.4-gallon fuel tank. Black 6.70
tubeless tires. White sidewall or nylon cord tires optional*. Vented chrome wheel covers with simulated knock-off hubs.
SPECIAL EQUIPMENT* FOR SPORTS CAR MEETS—RPO 687—Heavy-Duty Chassis Equipment includes special brakes with sintered-metallic facings, finned cast iron brake drums
built-in cooling fan, vented flange plates with air scoops, fast steering adapter for 16.3:1 overall ratio, heavy-duty front and rear shock absorbers**. RPO 276—Wide-base wheels with
rims (with hub caps instead of wheel covers). RPO 686—Special sintered-metallic brake linings. RPO 488—24-gallon fuel tank. RPO 441—off-the-road exhaust system.
BODY EXTERIOR—Fiber-glass reinforced plastic body—sculptured side and rear panels. Cove trim and rocker panel moldings. Magic-Mirror acrylic lacquer finish in seven solid co
Tuxedo Black, Ermine White, Roman Red, Sateen Silver, Almond Beige, Fawn Beige, Honduras Maroon. Front hinged hood. Three-unit front grille. Dual headlights in front fenders.
taillights. Push-button door handles and key lock. Cowl ventilator. Large luggage locker with spare wheel under floor. Concealed well for folding top behind seats. Choice of manu
operated folding soft top or easily removable plastic hard top (Second top optional*). Power-operated mechanism* for folding soft top. Frame-mounted wraparound bumpers.
INTERIOR FEATURES—Interior colors in black, red or fawn keyed to exterior colors. Foam-rubber padded all-vinyl bucket seats, individually adjustable. Safety belts. Long padded a
rest on each door. Recessed safety reflectors in door sidewall panels. Crank-operated windows, power-operated optional*. Vinyl-covered padded instrument panel. Passenger assist ba
instrument panel cove with stowage bin below. Pleated leather-grain vinyl sidewall trim. Carpeted floor, metal sills and step plates. Competition-type steering wheel. Speedometer, tachom
ammeter, fuel level, oil pressure and coolant temperature gauges, starter-ignition switch and light switch on instrument panel. Built-in, outside air heater-defroster with controls on ce
console. Directional signals, cigarette lighter, outside and inside rearview mirrors, dual electric link-driven windshield wipers, electric clock, parking brake alarm, courtesy light, right-
left-hand sunshades and push-button windshield washer. Ashtray, glove compartment with key lock located between seats. Transistorized signal-seeking radio* also available.
DIMENSIONS—Wheelbase, 102". Overall length, 176.7". Overall height: Soft top up, 52.2"; top down, 50.1"; hardtop 52.1". Height at door, 32.2". Road clearance, 6.7". Overall width, 7
Tread: front, 57"; rear, 59".

*optional at extra cost

1962 continued in the style of 1961. Minimal trim changes were made and these help the observer in differentiating the two. The big change for the year was the replacement of the former 283 cid engine with the new 327 V-8 with 4.0 inch pistons (vs 3.88) and a 3.25" stroke, a quarter of an inch longer. Compression ratio of the standard engine was raised to 10.5:1, these things providing the basic Corvette engine with a rating of 250 horsepower, almost 20% greater than 1961.

The revised rear end of 1961, and the new, larger engine of 1962, combine to explain Chevrolet's claim for 1962 of "new lines, new leap for America's Sports Car".

1962

1962 Corvette

Wind Wings are an owner-added accessory.

Mr. Herman Caruthers, El Cajon, California

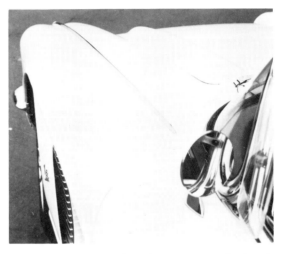

The long chrome stripe that starts at the head-lights continues along the top of the fenders almost to the windshield, paralleling the ridges on the hood.

The grill, formerly bright, is now anodized to a black finish emphasizing the air scoop effect. Above the grill is the name in block letters and a new front emblem.

This front emblem replaces the simp crossed flags of 1959. The emblem is n used again nor does it appear on the re deck.

Painted headlight bezels replaced the chromed units in 1961 adding to the appearance of the fenders. The chromed portion between the lights is a separate piece.

ere is no change in the front bumper or simulated scoop.

Parking light continues in its recess beneath the bumpers. As would be expected, these lights function as both marker lights and also directional signals.

The parking light lens is the same one used since 1954. The *housings*, however, are right and left-handed assemblies, and have been so since 1958 when they were first recessed.

The forward trim of the removable hard top has not changed since 1956. However, the tops are not interchangable (opposite page).

The new lightweight aluminum rocker panel moulding strip is extruded into a shape having a very sturdy appearance.

As well as a change in the side trim, a new rocker panel molding is added in 1962.

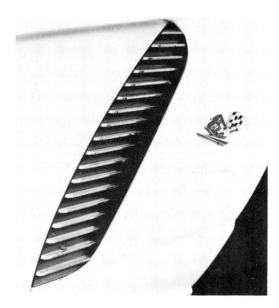

A new rendition of the crossed flags bearing a red, white, and blue bar, appears on the side of the 1962 model.

New short multiple trim bars replace the three stripes of 1961.

quick look at the rear identifies this as the
62 rather than 1961 model by the color of its
r deck emblem.

This emblem is identical with those used
from 1958 on except that the aluminum
backing plate has been painted black for
1962.

Due to the ridge in the rear deck lid which runs to the
cockpit, the lower edge of the tops are now recessed.
They are not, therefore, interchangable with those for
the 1956-1960 models.

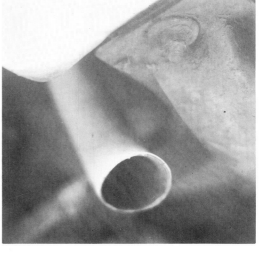

The dual exhaust system has been modified,
and starting with the 1961 model, they vent
on the sides, just ahead of the rear wheel well.

The redesigned rear end adds volume to the luggage compartment. Compare this view with that on page 131 of the earlier style.

A recessed tool storage area is provided in the rear de adjacent to the removable lid over the spare whe

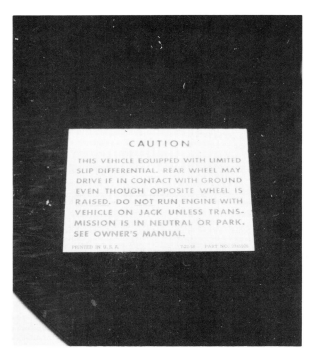

CAUTION

THIS VEHICLE EQUIPPED WITH LIMITED SLIP DIFFERENTIAL. REAR WHEEL MAY DRIVE IF IN CONTACT WITH GROUND EVEN THOUGH OPPOSITE WHEEL IS RAISED. DO NOT RUN ENGINE WITH VEHICLE ON JACK UNLESS TRANSMISSION IS IN NEUTRAL OR PARK. SEE OWNER'S MANUAL.

Positraction limited slip differential can cause the rear wheel on the ground to drive the car forward even if the other is jacked up. A warning against this condition is found on the access cover for the spare wheel.

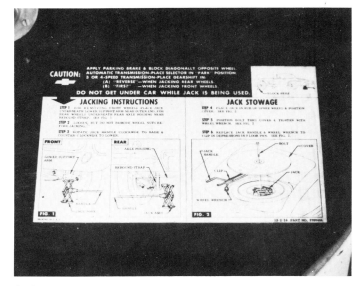

Jacking instructions also appear on the spare wheel access cover. Scissors, rather than bumper, jacks are standard in Corvettes.

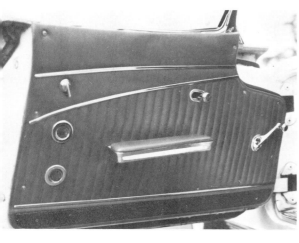

e trim of the door has again been changed, and features
ertical, rather than horizontal pattern.

Trim strips dress up the seams of previous year (page 146).

rtical pleated vinyl contrasts with metal
ing of previous years.

The reflectors in the door have
been changed, as has the arm rest,
and they are now placed one above
the other.

1962 is the last year for the competition type three spoke steering wheel which has been in use since 1956.

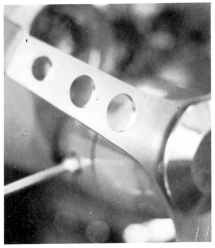

The foam rubber padded, vi covered bucket seats are indi ually adjustable. The rele lever for the driver's seat is n bottom of picture.

Interiors are available in black, red, or fawn (the blue of 1961 has been dropped). Resembling the pattern on the seats of the 1961 model, a difference is at the top where the pattern is carried up and over the crown.

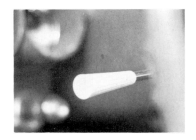

Beneath the grill is the speaker for the radio.

Ash trays are removable for emptying, and being symetrical, can be re-inserted either way. On the assumption that the unit is for the convenience of the driver, cars entered for judging are often penalized for such small matters as an ashtray "incorrectly" installed as shown here.

Speedomer is unchanged.

The use of this tachometer indicates the installation of one of the performance engines in this car. The standard engine, rated at 4400 rpm, would have been furnished with a tachometer red-lined at 5000 rpm.

The speedometer and gauges of the 1962 instrument panel are unchanged from their counterparts in 1961.

The 1961 Wonder Bar radio has not been changed, and is the only radio offered.

958 Corvette

otographed in Northridge, California in late 1957 by Glenn Embree

1954 Corvette

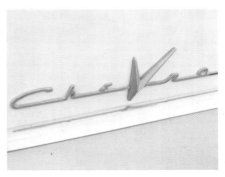

1955 Corvette

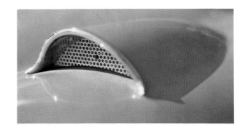

1956 Corvette

1957 Corvette

1958 Corvette

1959 Corvette

1960 Corvette

1961 Corvette

1962 Corvette

1963 Corvette Sting Ray Sport Coupe

1964 Corvette Sting Ray Convertible

1965 Corvette Sting Ray Sport Coupe

1966 Corvette Sting Ray Sport Coupe

1967 Corvette Sting Ray Convertible

1967 Corvette Sting Ray Sport Coupe

1968 Corvette Sting Ray Coupe

1969 Corvette Stingray Convertible

1970-71-72 Corvette Stingray Coupe (1970 illustrated)

1973-74-75 Corvette Stingray Coupe (1973 illustrated)

Again, the recessed instrument panel bears the Corvette name behind the grab rail.

The heater-defroster has become, in 1962, a standard equipment item and is no longer an extra cost option.

This barrel-shaped tank is the reservoir for the engine coolant. It is piped to the radiator and the overflow tube with light hose, and mounted on the left side of the block.

Introduced in 1961, the aluminum radiator was again used in 1962. Lighter than the copper radiator, and with a separate reservoir (left), it has no filler cap.

These cast aluminum valve covers are used on the high performance engines only. The standard engine had orange-painted steel covers with a decal, relating to the engine, of "327".

Fresh air for the Corvette heater-defroster is obtained through a flexible duct which scoops the air from the grill to avoid injesting engine fumes.

In 1961 and 1962, the serial number plate is placed under the hood at the bottom of the steering column.

The large flat buffed aluminum air cleaner contains an oil-wetted air filter.

The distributor shield is notched to clear the accelerator linkage. With only one carburetor here the throw is different in the linkage and the notch less pronounced than on dual-carburetor engines (page 137).

A glass bowl fuel filter is used at the intake to the four-barrel carburetor.

Rising past the valve cover on the right side is a tube which conducts heat from the exhaust manifold to the bi-metallic automatic choke on the carburetor.

NEW CORVETTE

SPECIFICATIONS

HP	Induction System	Comp. Ratio	Cam, Lifters	Distributor Points, Advance	Transmission	Rear Axle Ratio Std.	Positraction
250	4-Barrel Carburetor, Dual-Intake Air Cleaner	10.5:1	Std. Cam, Hydraulic Lifters	Single, Vacuum-Centrifugal	3-Speed	3.36:1	3.36:1
					4-Speed* (2.54:1 Low)	3.36:1†	3.08:1 3.36:1
					Powerglide*	3.36:1	3.36:1
300*	Large 4-Barrel Aluminum Body Carburetor, Dual-Intake Air Cleaner	10.5:1	Std. Cam, Hydraulic Lifters	Single, Vacuum-Centrifugal	3-Speed	3.36:1	3.36:1
					4-Speed* (2.54:1 Low)	3.36:1†	3.08:1 3.36:1
					Powerglide*	3.36:1	3.36:1
340*	Large 4-Barrel Aluminum Body Carburetor, High-Flow Air Cleaner	11.25:1	Special Cam, Mechanical Lifters	Single, Vacuum-Centrifugal	3-Speed	3.36:1	3.36:1
					4-Speed* (2.20:1 Low)	3.70:1	3.08:1 3.36:1 3.55:1 3.70:1 4.11:1 4.56:1
360*	Fuel Injection, Special Air Cleaner	11.25:1	Special Cam, Mechanical Lifters	Single, Vacuum-Centrifugal	3-Speed	3.36:1	3.36:1
					4-Speed* (2.20:1 Low)	3.70:1	3.08:1 3.36:1 3.55:1 3.70:1 4.11:1 4.56:1

† 3.08:1 Performance Cruise Ratio optional at extra cost.

*Optional at extra cost.

CORVETTE FEATURES FOR '63

Engines — All engines have independent mechanism for each valve; temperature controlled fan; precision-machined forged steel crankshaft; premium aluminum main bearings; full-pressure lubrication system; full flow oil filter; automatic choke; and a 12-volt electrical system. Oil-wetted polyurethane element in the air cleaner. All-aluminum cross-flow radiator. Positive closed-type crankcase ventilation.

Chassis — Direct double-acting freon-bag shock absorbers. Balanced steering linkage with 19.6:1 overall ratio can be reset to 17:1 (standard with power steering*). Hydraulic 11-inch brakes with fade-resistant bonded linings. Hand-operated parking brake on rear wheels. Black 6.70 x 15" tires standard. Optional* 6.70 x 15" nylon blackwalls or rayon whitewalls.

Exterior Features — Fiber-glass reinforced plastic body with Magic-Mirror acrylic lacquer finish in seven solid colors: Tuxedo Black, Ermine White, Riverside Red, Silver Blue, Daytona Blue, Saddle Tan and Sebring Silver*. Three Convertible tops (white, black and beige) available with any body color. Doors have push-button handles and key locks. Covered well for folding top behind seats.

Additional Optional Equipment* — Sintered-metallic brake linings. Cast aluminum wheels with 6" rims and knock-off hubs. Special performance equipment package (available only on the Sport Coupe with Fuel Injection engine, 4-Speed transmission and Positraction) includes: power-type heavy-duty brakes including finned drums with built-in fans, vented backing plates and front brake air scoops, special sintered-metallic linings and self-adjusting feature when driving forward; dual-circuit brake master cylinder; heavy-duty stabilizer bar; 36-gallon fuel tank; heavy-duty front and springs and shock absorbers; aluminum wheels with 6" rims and knock-off hubs. *Optional at extra*

Dimensions — Wheelbase, 98". Overall length, 175.3". Overall height Convertible with soft top up, 49.8"; Convertible with optional hard 49.3"; Sport Coupe, 49.8". Cowl height to ground, 34.9". Door open height to ground: Convertible, 45.5"; Sport Coupe, 46.7". Road cleara 5.0". Overall width, 69.6". Tread: front; 56.3"; rear 57.0".

il 1963, Corvette had been essentially an open car for which a buyer could obtain a folding soft top or a removable hard top (or h). If the hard top gave the impression of a truly enclosed automobile, so be it, but the <u>fact</u> is that it was still only an open car a fitted top. Not after 1963, however, for in that year, in addition to continuing the previous concept, Corvette was presented rnately in a closed version of considerable style.

new model was a coupe of entirely new appearance. Later to become known as a "Fastback" due to the smooth transition of lines of the roof to the rear, it was introduced with a new name, the "Corvette Sting Ray Sport Coupe". The open car with re- able or foldable top was continued, of course, and for the first time obtained a name of its own, the "Corvette Sting Ray Con- ible".

1963 Sting Ray introduced for the first time a full four-wheel independent suspension (earlier cars had independently sus- ded front wheels only), adjustable steering columns, wider wheel rims, and a continuation of the excellently received 327 hp nes first used on the 1962 model. With innovations including optional power steering and brakes, and much that was new in interiors, the 1963 model was indeed a "New Corvette".

1963 Sting Ray Sport Coupe

Mr. George McDonald, San Diego, California

The new look for the Corvette is emphasized by a sha
sloping hood which dips below the fender line.

Headlights, ordinarily concealed, rotate into position
in response to a switch under
the instrument panel. The
headlight housing, like the
body, is made of plastic.

This new version of the crossed flags appears
on the front of the car.

he new look of the hood is highlighted by a long arrow-
aped feature flanked by two vent-like simulations.

These plastic grills are dummys, and are set into a
recess in the solid hood. They are added for appearance only.

Beneath the new bumper can be seen a portion
of a new horizontally-lined aluminum grill.

Parking lights are ringed with a chromed
bezel and placed at either side of the grill.
For the first time, amber lenses are
furnished for improved visibility.

The rear compartment of the Sport Coupe is nicely carpeted and is quite adequate for luggage or even extra passengers.

The 1963 Sting Ray Convertible is again offered with a choice of folding soft top or removable hard top (or optionally, both). The lines, of the hard top have been changed though, and the former quarter windows are now omitted.

wide plastic rear window gives excellent rear sion on the Convertible.

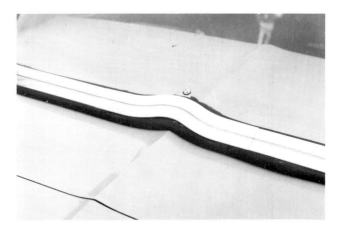

As previously, the bottom of the removable tops must be notched to clear a reinforcing ridge down the center of the back of the car.

The new wheel covers have "spinners" simulating knock-off wheel hubs.

Fuel Injection, a popular option, is continued, and when installed, is identified with this nameplate placed on the sides of the car in addition to the standard emblem (below).

When fuel injection is not installed, the decoration on the sides is limited to this emblem.

In addition to those in front, the rear fenders also crown sharply for added effect.

A new outside door handle and keylock are introduced in 1963, ending the run of the earlier sty (page 72) that was employed from 1956 throug 1962.

wrap-around windshield, so long a Corvette
emark, is eliminated in 1963.

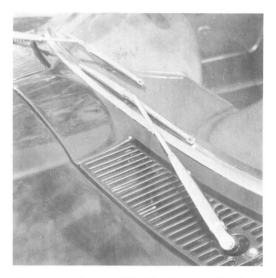

Long, oversize windshield wipers overlap for
best coverage.

ew "ventipanes" are crank operated (below)
d open to provide ventilation on both models
the new Sting Ray.

A new windshield washer is standard this
year.

Early in the model year, the 1963 Corvettes were equipped with conventional
passenger car mirrors (below). About
mid-year, the new unique Corvette mirror
(left) was introduced and persisted
through 1967.

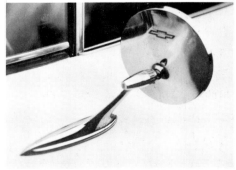

Although unseen, a steel "bird cage" framework beneath plastic shell of the Sting Ray adds to the structural integ of the body.

These dummy vents are for effect only and do not open to admit or vent air.

Chrome strips encircle the halves of the rear window.

The doors of the Coupe extend up and curve over into the top for a greatly improved accessibility.

The highly unique feature of the 1963 Corvette Sting Ray Coupe—the "split" rear window.

e gas filler cap located on the center line
the back, has a spring-loaded roller latch.

The Sting Ray name is incorporated into an emblem on the rear of the car.

New wide bumpers wrap around the corners of the car.

The radio antenna is mounted near the back of the left rear fender.

A new location for the spare wheel takes it under the rear deck with access only from the outside. A tray, hinged at the front, is provided which drops to accept the wheel. When elevated, the tray is held in place by a hex-headed bolt.

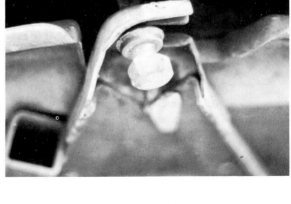

An accessory lock is available to prevent theft of the spare wheel.

Steering wheel muff is an owner-installed accessory.

Seats are upholstered in a pattern of narrow pleats ringed by a comfortable bolster. The interiors are color-keyed to the outside and are furnished in black, red, dark blue, and saddle colored leather-grained vinyl. For the first time, an optional genuine leather interior is offered.

The 1963 Corvette had a recessed chamber under the driver's seat in which small tools could be kept. During the later part of the model year this was omitted.

This dome light is furnished in the coupe.

The interior view of the 1963 "split window" cou
displays the section which blocks rear vision. Mar
coupes were later modified to eliminate the pillar bu
curiously, unmodified cars have now become high
interesting collector's items.

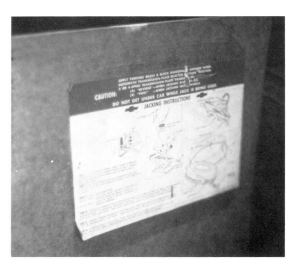

Two compartments under the floor provide storage.
Under the lid of one is a sheet with the jacking instructions, and the conventional scissors jack.

New for 1963 is a black door knob
replacing the white ones used since
1956.

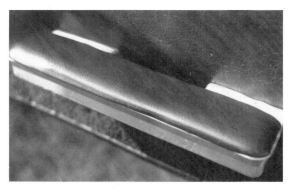

Arm rests, similar to those first used in 1962, are
repeated in the 1963 model.

Safety reflectors are again place
in the doors to be illuminated b
oncoming traffic when the do
is open. This is the upper o
which *also* functions as the i
side door lock.

The new steering wheel introduced in 1963 has three formed spring steel slotted spokes so arranged that the upper quadrant provides clear view of the instrument panel. The hub of the wheel is recessed for safety purposes and fitted with a distinctive horn button. A new feature is an adjustable steering column.

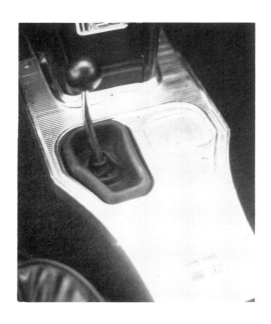

w for 1963 is this black ar shift lever knob. A bber boot is provided the base of the lever.

Optional power windows, when selected, are controlled by switches on the console.

A new, round, speedometer on the left is matched with a new 7000 rpm tachometer for excellent effec
Red-lined at 5000 rpm, this is the tachometer furnished with the standard engine. Optional High Perfo
mance engines call for higher warning levels up to the 360 HP fuel injection engine which comes with
warning buzzer coupled to the tachometer.

Suspended beneath the instrument panel on the left side is a new hood release knob and a control for incoming air. On the instrument panel is a light switch (below), an ammeter, and the windshield wiper washer control.

At the right side of the instrument cluster is an oil gauge and a new ignition switch (page 160) now having a position for the operation of accessories without engine operation.

The headlights are controlled both by a light switch (upper) which illuminates them, and also a second switch (lower) to operate the electric motors used to revolve the lights into position (page 184).

A new storage space is presented in the 1963 Corvette in the form of a lockable compartment behind this hinged cover. The cover itself is also made of the fiber glass reinforced plastic of the body with the Sting Ray emblem molded in.

Identification data is now placed on plates riveted to the body beneath the glove compartment door.

A new electric clock is placed at the top of the center divider where it is easier to read.

ne other optional radio available 1963 is the signal-seeking Won- r Bar model which for 1963 bears e name CORVETTE on the ning bar.

For the first time, an AM/FM radio is offered optionally in the Corvette. By sliding the bar at the left of the tuning face up (right) the AM dial is exposed and circuits activated and the letters AM appear in the window below the bar.

Corvette hoods are hinged at the front and open from the rear to allow engine access.

Spring-loaded bumpers are placed at the corners of the hood and when closed, their cone-shaped tips are secured by latches. A handle placed under the instrument panel withdraws the latches to open the hood.

A latching bracket at one side holds the hood in the open position.

In a regrettable move, several years ago many 1963 Sting Ray Coupes were modified and updated by having their rear window center section removed and a later Sting Ray rear window (and trim) installed. For this reason, and since the split window was only used in this one model year, the unmodified 1963 Sting Ray Coupe appears to be commanding a higher Collector value than the similar, but later, models.

"A Sports Car with a Dual Personality"

SPECIFICATIONS

Aluminum Wide-Rim Wheels* with Knock-off Hubs

HP	CORVETTE POWER TEAMS Induction System	Comp. Ratio	Cam Lifters	Distributor Points, Advance	Trans- mission	Rear Axle Ratio Std.	*Posi- traction
250	4-Barrel Car- buretor, Dual- Intake Air Cleaner	10.5:1	Std. Cam, Hydraulic Lifters	Single, Vacuum- Centrifugal	3-Speed	3.36:1	3.36:1
					4-Speed* (2.56:1 Low)	3.36:1†	3.08:1 3.36:1
					Powerglide*	3.36:1	3.36:1
300*	Large 4-Barrel Carburetor, Dual-Intake Air Cleaner	10.5:1	Std. Cam, Hydraulic Lifters	Single, Vacuum- Centrifugal	3-Speed	3.36:1	3.36:1
					4-Speed* (2.56:1 Low)	3.36:1†	3.08:1 3.36:1
					Powerglide*	3.36:1	3.36:1
365*	Special 4-Barrel Carburetor, High-Flow Air Cleaner	11.0:1	Special Cam, Mechanical Lifters	Single, Vacuum- Centrifugal	3-Speed	3.36:1	3.36:1
					4-Speed* (2.20:1 Low)	3.70:1	3.08:1 3.36:1 3.55:1 3.70:1 4.11:1 4.56:1
375*	Fuel Injection, Special Air Cleaner	11.0:1	Special Cam, Mechanical Lifters	Single, Vacuum- Centrifugal	3-Speed	3.36:1	3.36:1
					4-Speed* (2.20:1 Low)	3.70:1	3.08:1 3.36:1 3.55:1 3.70:1 4.11:1 4.56:1

*Optional at extra cost.   †3.08:1 Performance Cruise Ratio optional at extra cost.

Engines—All engines have independent mechanism for each valve; temperature-controlled fan; precision-machined forged steel crankshaft; premium aluminum main bearings; full-pressure lubrication system; full-flow oil filter; auto-matic choke; and a 12-volt electrical system. Oil-wetted polyurethane air cleaner element. All-aluminum cross-flow radiator. Positive closed-type crankcase ventilation.

Chassis—Direct double-acting freon-bag shock absorbers. Balanced steering linkage with 19.6:1 overall ratio can be reset to 17:1 (standard with power steering*). Hydraulic 11-inch brakes with fade-resistant bonded linings. Hand-operated parking brake. Black 6.70 x 15″ tires standard. Optional* 6.70 x 15″ nylon blackwalls or rayon whitewalls.

Exterior Features—Fiber glass reinforced plastic body with Magic-Mirror acrylic lacquer finish in seven solid colors: Tuxedo Black, Ermine White, Riverside Red, Silver Blue, Daytona Blue, Saddle Tan and Satin Silver. Three Con-vertible tops (white, black and beige) available with any body color. Doors have push-button handles and key locks.

Covered space for folding top behind seats.

Additional Optional Equipment—Back-up lights, sintered metallic brake linings. Cast aluminum wheels with 6″ rim and knock-off hubs. 36.5-gallon fuel tank (Sport Coupe only). Off-road exhaust system. Full-transistor ignition system (available only on 365- and 375-hp engines). Special performance equipment grouping (with 375-hp engine, 4-Speed transmission and Positraction) offers special power brakes with finned drums, built-in cooling fans, front brake air scoops, special sintered-metallic linings, and forward-driving self-adjusting feature; dual circuit brake master cylinder; heavy-duty stabilizer bar; heavy-duty front and rear springs and shock absorbers.

Dimensions—Wheelbase, 98″. Overall length, 175.3″. Overall height: Convertible with soft top up, 49.8″; Convertible with hardtop, 49.3″; Sport Coupe, 49.8″. Cowl height to ground, 34.9″. Door opening height to ground: Convertible, 45.6″; Sport Coupe, 46.8″. Road clearance, 5.0″. Overall width, 69.6″. Tread: front, 56.3″; rear 57.0″.

...vette Sting Ray Convertible with Removable Hard Top.

...ddition to pointing out its reputation for performance, in 1964 Corvette's sales folders took on lesser known features of special ...rest which added another side to its personality. Doors were recessed into the roof, said the brochure, to permit better access to ...gile feminine coiffures"; the elimination of the split rear window gave "lady buffs . . . great hindsight without straining in their ...s", and new more "tasteful" rocker panels were claimed.

...s initial appeal to the distaff side not withstanding, the encouraging results of the first year of the Coupe's existence (at 49.2% ...y almost matched the sales of the Convertible) were not continued and the Coupe drew to only a 37% showing for the year. As ...atter of fact, it is surprising to note that not until 1969 was the Coupe ever to outsell the Convertible.

...nges for 1964 included a new set of variable rate springs for softer and better ride, and an increase in rated output of the two ...engines. To reduce noise, added rubber insolators were provided. Thus the car went forward with its initial sports car road-...dling characteristics and at the same time incorporated refinements offering a bit more in the way of "luxury". Thus the claim ...de in 1964 that Corvette is "a sports car with dual personality".

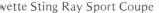

...vette Sting Ray Sport Coupe

1964 Corvette Sting Ray Sport Coupe

Mr. Bob Wingate, Glendora, California

The crown in the fenders is typical of this series of Corvette.

The ridge down the center of the hood, called a "windsplit" by Chevrolet serves the useful purpose of reinforcing the hood.

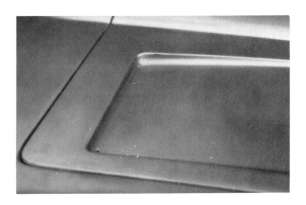

For 1964, although the recesses are retained, the simulated grills of 1963 (page 185) are eliminated.

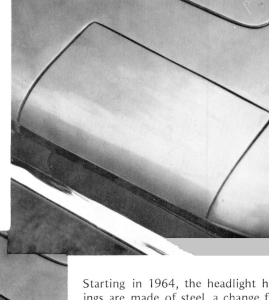

The crossed flag insignia remains on the front of the hood.

Starting in 1964, the headlight housings are made of steel, a change from the plastic "buckets" of 1963.

w wheelcovers appear for 1964. Early in the
ir the smooth section is satin finish, but
rtly this is replaced with the glossy chromed
ish shown here.

Front bumpers are made to wrap protectively around the fender and to
protect the amber parking light below
it.

There is no change in the *appearance* of this emblem or its location
on the fenders, but a change in its
thickness made during 1963 makes
it unique to the later models. See
page 286.

A new rocker panel moulding (page 188) has
fewer, and wider, stripes.

The two simulated vents in the front
fenders are unchanged.

in 1963, an aluminum grill featuring
izontal lines is used.

New for 1964 is a working ventilation system in the Sport Coupe. Operated by a switch on the instrument panel near the headlight-rotating switch, the system functions only when the heater is OFF. A blower mounted in the body side panel behind the driver's seat draws air out of the compartment through these louvered openings.

Only a quick look at the vents establishes that this not the 1963 model (page 190).

This outside rear view mirror was introduced during 1963 and remains standard through the 1967 model.

The inside rear view mirror is mounted on a graceful arm.

improved visibility, the rear window of the 1964 Sting Ray Coupe
ts the divider of the 1963 model.

Late in 1963, a change was made in the design of this new gas tank filler lid (page 181).

The emblem on the rear deck is unchanged.

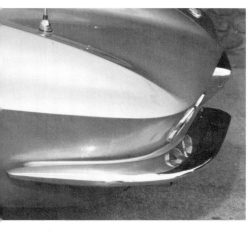

protective wrap-around bumpers are con-
ued in 1964.

Optional back-up lights, when installed, are placed in the inner pair of the four standard tail lights and a clear lens furnished instead of red.

All-new chromed inside door knobs appear for the first time on 1964 Corvette door.

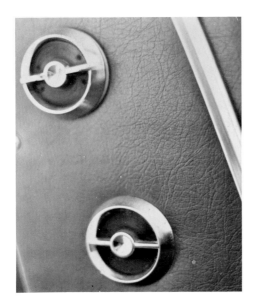

Two safety reflectors are again furnished on each door.

The "ventipanes" are crank-operated, and the cranks are carried over from 1963.

Although sized as previously, the 1964 inside door knobs are chromed rather than simply plastic globes.

The standard window cranks are similar those on the vent windows. If the po option is purchased, they are omit

Resembling the similar view of the 1963 model, the 1964 Corvette has subtle differences such as a change in the instrument faces and a new standard walnut-finish steering wheel rim.

Although the instruments are shaped the same, their dials are finished differently. A pattern of concentric rings starting at the center replaces the solid inner ring of 1963.

The layout of the control console is unchanged.

Seats are individually adjustable and each is furnished with a latching knob.

A minor change in the upholstery provides slightly wider and more comfortable bolsters although the pleated center portion appears unchanged. 1964 interiors are furnished in Black, Red, Dark Blue, Silver, White, or Saddle Vinyl and full leather interiors are an option.

1964

Standard for 1964 is a new simulated-walnut steering wheel rim. The directional signal lever knob is chrome finished to match other trim for the year.

The ignition lock is changed to a less costly stamping but its functions are unchanged.

Air Conditioning became an option in 1963. Three vents are provided, one in the console above the clock, and an adjustable sphere just below each end of the instrument panel. The face of the new clock matches the other instruments and also bears the pattern of concentric circles.

The center console contains radio, heater and controls, clock, and, when installed, air conditioning controls and vent.

New chromed knobs are provided for the gear shift lever, and a new rubber boot serves better to seal the shift lever. This is the 4-speed transmission, furnished with a mechanical lock to prevent inadvertent reverse shifts.

This chromed knob is placed on an automatic transmission; the reverse lock-out release is not used as it is with the 4-speed (photo above).

Controls for the optional power windows remain on the console. By now Powerglide automatic transmission has the P-R-N-D-L sequence adopted almost universally by automobile manufacturers.

Only one radio is offered for 1964. This is an AM/FM radio with five push buttons. Manufactured by the Delco division of GM, they nevertheless did vary somewhat as will be noted by a glance at the dial calibrations of two 1964 Corvette radios.

The cowl over the glove compartment door is slotted to provide a hand hold.

From 1964 on, the earlier plastic glove box door is replaced with a metal stamping. The trim and the emblem are now added pieces, no longer cast into the door as they were in 1963.

Incoming air is ducted to vents at either side of the central console.

The lines of the Sting Ray Convertible, even when fitted with a removable hard top, differ from those of the Coupe.

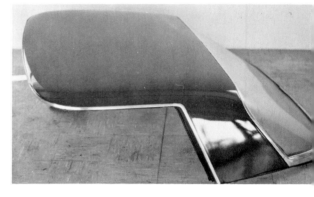

The removable hard top is a light weight plastic part with bright metal trim. The rear window is also plastic.

The wide rear window of the removable hard top offers excellent visibility plus a sporty effect quite different from that of the Coupe.

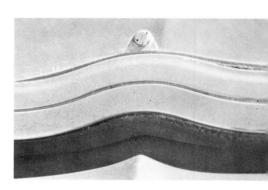

The lower edge of the tops has been recessed to clear the characteristic center ridge on the body.

Beneath the rear deck, but accessible only from the interior, is a storage area (next page).

214

Headlining in the removable hard top is smooth finished vinyl.

The dual sun visors (standard only since 1963) are secured to the windshield frame, not the top.

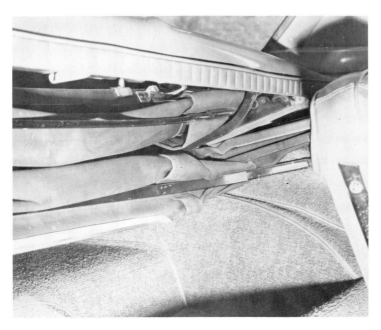

Beneath the fixed rear deck is a storage space for a folded soft top. These are available in white, black, or beige. Below the hump in the floor under the top is the gasoline tank in its conventional Corvette location.

In addition to the top storage area, the Convertible also has a small luggage area behind the seats.

1965

"A True All-American Sports Car"

SPECIFICATIONS

STING RAY POWER TEAMS

Some Available Options:

. . . Heavy-Duty Suspension
. . . Side-Mounted Exhaust System
. . . Positraction Limited Slip Differential
. . . Power Brakes
. . . Telescopic Steering Column
. . . Power Steering
. . . Whitewall Tires
. . . Cast Aluminum Wheels
. . . 36 gallon Fuel Tank (Sport Coupe only)
. . . Transistor Ignition
. . . 300 hp, 350 hp, 365 hp, or 375 hp engine
. . . 4-speed, or 4-speed close radio, or Powerglide transmission
. . . Tinted Glass
. . . Back-up Lights
. . . Air Conditioning
. . . Leather Seat Upholstery
. . . Wood-rimmed Steering Wheel
. . . Electric Windows
. . . AM/FM Radio with remote control power antenna
. . . Removable Hard Top (Convertible only) Etc.

ENGINE BORE & STROKE	HORSEPOWER & TORQUE	INDUCTION SYSTEM	C.R.	CAM & LIFTERS	TRANS-MISSIONS	AXLE RATIOS STD.	POSI-TRACTION
STANDARD ENGINE							
327 cu. in. V8 4.00 x 3.25 in.	250 @ 4400 350 @ 2800	4-BBL Carburetor Dual-Intake Air Cleaner	10.5:1	General Purpose Hydraulic	3-Speed 2.58:1 first	3.36:1	3.36:1
					4-Speed 2.56:1 first	3.36:1*	3.08:1 3.36:1
					Powerglide	3.36:1	3.36:1
EXTRA-COST OPTIONAL ENGINES							
327 cu. in. V8 4.00 x 3.25 in.	300 @ 5000 360 @ 3200	Large 4-BBL Carburetor Dual-Intake Air Cleaner	10.5:1	General Purpose Hydraulic	4-Speed 2.56:1 first	3.36:1*	3.08:1 3.36:1
					Powerglide	3.36:1	3.36:1
327 cu. in. V8 4.00 x 3.25 in.	350 @ 5800 360 @ 3600	Special 4-BBL Carburetor High-Flow Air Cleaner	11.0:1	General Purpose Hydraulic	4-Speed 2.20:1 first	3.70:1	3.08:1 3.36:1 3.55:1 4.11:1 4.56:1
327 cu. in. V8 4.00 x 3.25 in.	365 @ 6200 350 @ 4000	Special 4-BBL Carburetor High-Flow Air Cleaner	11.0:1	Special Purpose Mechanical	4-Speed 2.20:1 first	3.70:1	3.08:1 3.36:1 3.55:1 4.11:1 4.56:1
327 cu. in. V8 4.00 x 3.25 in.	375 @ 6200 350 @ 44-4800	Ramjet Fuel Injection Special Air Cleaner	11.0:1	Special Purpose Mechanical	4-Speed 2.20:1 first	3.70:1	3.08:1 3.36:1 3.55:1 4.11:1 4.56:1

*3.08:1 Performance Cruise axle ratio can be specified.

tle changed from its predecessors, the 1965 Sting Ray has their best features plus a new four-wheel disc brake system. A long list
optional features permit the equipping of a car to personal preferences and a good number of these options are in the performance
d including close-ratio 4-speed transmission, and additional engine refinements. During the later part of the year, an even greater
wer source appears with the introduction of the big block Turbo-Jet 396 cubic inch engine which called for the use of a formidible
v hood to conceal its increased height.

w colors for 1965 are Silver Pearl, Rally Red, Milano Maroon, Nassau Blue, Goldwood Yellow, and Glen Green in addition to the
lier Tuxedo Black and Ermine White. As previously, acrylic laquer paints are used enabling subsequent touch-up and repair with
aimum difficulty.

h its full four-wheel independent suspension, its disc brakes, and its standard 250 horsepower engine, even the standard three-speed
nsmission gives a satisfying sense of power. With options ranging all the way to a 375 horsepower fuel-injected engine and fast
se-ratio 4-speed transmission, the car certainly is "a true All-American sports car".

55 Corvette Sting Ray Sport Coupe   *Mrs. Jill Pono, Oceanside, California*

The new fender louvers have been redesigned as functional items. By venting air brought through the engine compartment, they serve to improve cooling. Below them appears a new smooth-finish rocker panel moulding.

A new front grill pattern features a rectangular pattern.

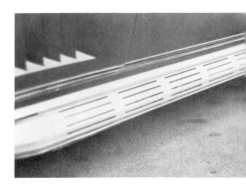

Shown here mounted on a 1967, an optic Side Mounted exhaust system was introduc in 1965 and continued through 1967 changed.

The exhaust blower system introduced
in 1964 continues through 1965 and then
is eliminated.

The two recesses in the hood, originally provided to house
the simulated vents of 1963 are finally eliminated entirely
for a much smoother appearance in 1965.

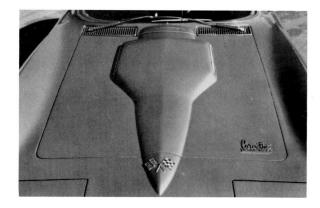

During 1965, the new Turbo-Jet 396 cid big block
engine became available in the Corvette, replacing
Fuel Injection in the top performance engine option.
For this bigger engine a new hood was provided with
a wider section better to clear its air cleaner.

The characteristic windsplit line down the center of Sting Ray splits the roof of the Coupe.

The single-pane curved rear window is continued unchanged.

The fuel filler access cover bears a distinctive new design.

Back up lights are an option and when selected are placed in the inner pair of the four rear lights.

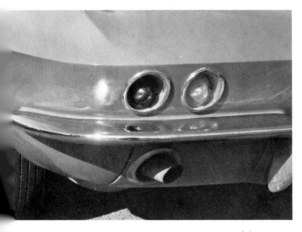

here is no change in the rear wrap-around bumper.

Again the dual exhaust exits through the body via a chromed bezel. Corvette exhaust pipes have a characteristic beveled rear end to aid in directing exhaust away from the body.

This is the last year for this script. A new one will appear in 1966.

A new horn button appears in 1965. On it the Corvette name is deleted (page 210).

In addition to two-tone interiors in silver/black, black, white/black, white/red, and white/blue, there are also maroon, green, black, red, blue, and saddle, all available as standard choices. In addition, there is a full-leather seat interior.

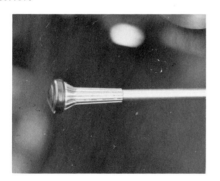

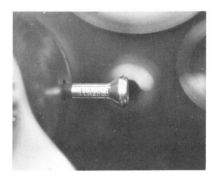

A new option this year is an emergency warning switch to flash the marker lights if needed.

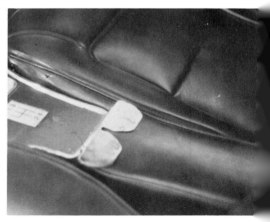

These clips are provided to secure unused seat belt buckles.

The four-speed transmissions are again provided with a mechanicanism to avoid inadvertent Reserve shifts.

When selected, the optional electric power-operated windows are controlled from switches placed on the console. Powerglide, another optional transmission has its own shift pattern displayed when selected, and this year, for the first time, it is presented with a straight-line pattern.

Lamps placed behind the rectangular windows flash to illuminate a warning for LIGHTS (left) or BRAKE (right). The LAMP light indicates a closed headlight "door" when the lights are turned on. Both warning lights operate only with the ignition switch in the ON position.

brings a new revision of the dial faces on the instruments in which the inner section of concentric circles (e 209) is deleted.

The tachometer is red-lined at 5000 for the standard engine, but the 350 hp 325, and larger engines, are red-lined at 6500.

The gauges are, like the instruments above, cleaner in appearance having lost the concentric trim.

A new 24 hour dial appears on the standard electric clock, and for the sports-minded, a sweep-second hand.

THE 1966 CORVETTE STING-RAY BY CHEVROLET

Features and Options and all that's new

Some Available "luxury" Options:

. . . Air Conditioning
. . . Genuine Leather Seat Trim
. . . Day/Night Inside Rear View Mirror
. . . Tinted Glass
. . . AM/FM Including rear-mounted Po[wer]
     Antenna
. . . Folding Soft Top or Removable H[ard]
     Top for Convertibles
. . . Power Windows
. . . Power Brakes
. . . Power Steering
. . . Telescopic Steering Wheel
. . . Teakwood Steering Wheel
. . . Emergency Road Kit (Flares, fire [ex]
     tinguisher, etc.)
. . . Whitewall Tires
. . . Powerglide Automatic Transmission
. . . Traffic Hazard Warning
. . . Deck Lid Luggage Carrier

SPECIFICATIONS

Some Available "off-road" Options:

. . . 425 hp Turbo-Jet 427
. . . 4-speed Transmission
. . . Heavy-Duty Brakes
. . . Positraction Limited Slip Differential
. . . Special Suspension
. . . Aluminum Wheels
. . . Side Mounted Exhaust
. . . 36 Gallon Fuel Tank
. . . Transistor Ignition

1966 CORVETTE POWER TEAM CHART

Engine Bore & Stroke	Horsepower & Torque at RPM	Carburetion & Induction System	Comp. Ratio	Cam & Lifters	Transmission	Axle Ratios Standard	Axle Ratios Positraction
STANDARD ENGINE							
327-cu.-in. V8	300 @ 5000	4-Barrel	10.5:1	General Purpose	3-Speed 2.54:1 first	3.36:1	3.08:1 3.36:1
				Hydraulic	4-Speed 2.52:1 first	3.36:1	3.08:1 3.36:1
4.00 x 3.25 in.	360 @ 3200	High-Flow Air Cleaner			Powerglide	3.36:1	3.36:1
EXTRA-COST OPTIONAL ENGINES							
327-cu.-in. V8	350 @ 5800	4-Barrel	11.0:1	High Performance	4-Speed 2.52:1 first	3.36:1	3.36:1 3.55:1
4.00 x 3.25 in.	360 @ 3600	High-Flow Air Cleaner		Hydraulic	4-Speed 2.20:1 first	3.70:1	3.70:1 4.11:1
427-cu.-in. V8	390 @ 5200	4-Barrel	10.25:1	High Performance	4-Speed 2.52:1 first	Positraction only 3.08:1	3.36:1
4.25 x 3.76 in.	460 @ 3600	High-Flow Air Cleaner		Hydraulic	4-Speed 2.20:1 first	Posit. only 3.36:1	3.08:1 3.70:1
427-cu.-in. V8	425 @ 5600	Large 4-Barrel	11.0:1	Special Performance	4-Speed 2.20:1 first	Posit. only 3.55:1	3.36:1 3.70:1 4.11:1
4.25 x 3.76 in.	460 @ 4000	High-Flow Air Cleaner		Mechanical	Heavy-Duty 4-Speed† 2.20:1 first	Specify from list at right	3.08:1 3.36:1 3.55:1 3.70:1 4.11:1 4.56:1

†Not recommended for general driving.

Much that was the 1965 Corvette returned to become the 1966 model, but not quite everything. Neither was the 1966
all-new model. Gone were the vents at the side of the quarter panel of the Sting Ray Coupe, and new was the rocker panel
the fender vents. Also new were some exterior colors (Laguna Blue and Trophy Blue) and shading and color differences
ting in a new yellow (Sunfire Yellow) and green (Mosport Green) exterior finishes. The other colors of 1965 (Tuxedo
k, Ermine White, Rally Red, Nassau Blue, Silver Pearl, and Milano Maroon) were continued through this year.

The big news for 1966 however was the optional new big block 427 engine. The standard engine, a 300 horsepower 327
V-8 was joined for the first time with a pair of optional 427 cid engines ranging up to 425 horsepower, (achieved without
injection which had been discontinued during 1965). These bigger engines featured larger (4.25") bore, longer (3.76")
ke, extra wide main bearing caps, and a five main-bearing crankshaft. With bigger valves and high lift camshafts, these
nes represented a great deal more than was previously available and although they required a special hood incorpor-
a stylized cavity to clear the air cleaner, they were thought well enough of to quickly become a popular option.

The Standard engine for the year, the reliable 327 was available in two versions to match the two choices of the 427.
cally rated at 300 horsepower, it could be optionally boosted to 350 hp at comparatively little cost. Although the 396
engine offered for a time in 1965 had been discontinued, the 427 cid engine, basically rated at 390, was also available in
5 hp version. It is these two latter options that explain Corvettes claim in 1966 of "two brand-new Turbo-Jet V-8's".

1966 Corvette Sting Ray Sport Coupe

Mrs. Bonnie Woodbury, Cardiff, California

A new grill which features a rectangular mesh appears on the 1966 thus changing the frontal appearance.

The familiar wrap-around bumpers remain unchanged.

The standard Corvette wheel covers for 1966 are chromed and again feature a three spoke spinner. Optional cast aluminum knock-off quick change wheels (left) have a 6" rim to accommodate wider tires.

The 327 standard engine, and the optional 350 hp version of it, were covered by the familiar Corvette hood (page 219) introduced in 1965.

Bright grill inserts on the hood sides provides air passage better to cool the new big engines.

The familiar Corvette crossed flags are used on the front regardless of hood choice.

The wider tires used on the aluminum wheels appear prominent in this view.

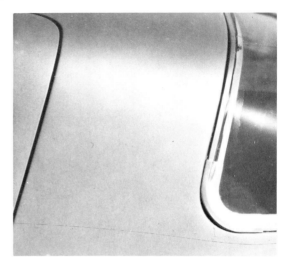

As the system has been discarded, no cowl ventilator grill appears on the Sport Coupe.

As in 1965, a pattern of three vents appear at the front fender sides.

This handsome new emblem is placed above the fender grills if the optional 427 cid engine is selected. If not, the crossed flag emblem (page 205) appears.

Again in 1966 a new rocker panel moulding furnished. In place of the smooth moulding of 1965 (page 218), a new seven-slot aluminum trim is provided.

The popular one piece wrap-around rear window remains unchanged from the previous year.

The fuel filler cap design is changed again for 1966.

The inclinded script of the previous years has been changed and for 1966 the trim on the rear deck is more erect (page 221).

ck up lights, until now optional, are now ndard items.

A new molded inside door covering appears in 1966 which features a longer arm rest. The reflectors, for so long a feature of the doors (page 208), were eliminated in 1965.

If the optional power windows are selected, the side window regulator handle (below) would be omitted, but the vent window crank (above) would remain as vents are not power-operated.

A chromed knob is used on the inside door latch release.

The separate inside door lock reappeared in 1965, and is this year used again.

New in 1966 is this handle plac[ed] carefully to aid in closing the do[or]

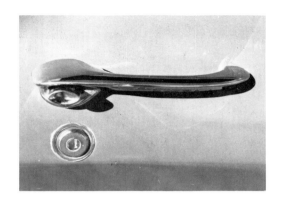

design of the doors of the Sport Coupe is
changed and they still curve neatly into the
f to provide better accessibility.

Power Brakes are an option commemorated by
this special brake pedal.

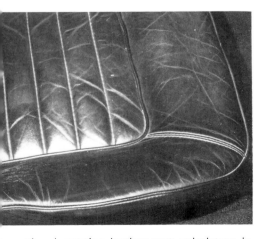

eriors are furnished in black, red, bright blue,
dle, silver, green, blue, and white/blue, the largest
or choice to date.

Seats are upholstered in a pattern of horizontal lines
encircled by the bolsters.

e optional genuine leather seat upholstery is
ilable in most of the above colors.

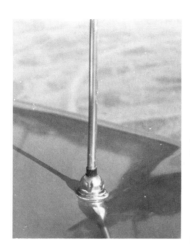

Another option in 1966 is a power-operated rear-mounted antenna controlled by this switch suspended below the instrument panel.

An option, first offered in 1966, is this inside non-glare rear view mirror.

First introduced in 1965, the genuine teakwood rim steering wheel is again offered as an option in 1966.

An optional telescopic steering column was offered. Its locking hub, which adjusted through a 3" travel, surrounds this horn button unique to this device. Note the red, white, and blue segments in the circle surrounding the "bowtie" insignia.

The new 427 cid engine calls for this tachometer which is redlined at 6500 rpm. Standard 327 engines would use the one shown previously (page 223).

...bove, and to the right, of the ...uel gauge is a light which con-...rms left directional signalling.

Matching it, above the temperature gauge, is another for right turns.

A locking storage compartment is again provided.

The new erect script is also used on the storage compartment lid.

These ducts direct the warm air from the heater to the base of the console.

"Luxury or a Sports Car . . . It's Both"

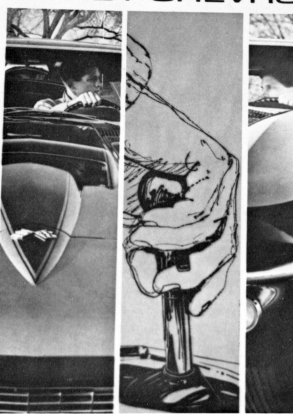

'67 Corvette BY CHEVROLET

EXTRA-COST OPTIONS AND CUSTOM FEATURES* TO MAKE DRIVING A CORVETTE EVEN MORE PLEASURABLE

350-hp Turbo-Fire 327; 390-, 400- or 435-hp Turbo-Jet 427. An automatic Powerglide or 4-Speed fully synchronized transmission. Four-Season air conditioning. Power brakes, power steering, power windows. AM/FM pushbutton radio. Removable hardtop for convertible. Black vinyl roof cover for removable hardtop. Positraction rear axle. Leather seat trim. Shoulder belts. Whitewall or red-stripe tires. Soft-Ray tinted windows and/or windshield. Full-transistor ignition system (not available with standard engine). Heavy-duty brakes. Special-performance front and rear suspension. Off-road exhaust system (not available with Powerglide). Dual side-mounted off-road exhausts. Telescopic steering wheel. Emergency road kit. Compass. Gas tank filler cap lock. Removable floor mats. 36.5-gallon gas tank for sport coupe only. Convertible deck lid luggage carrier plus strap. Convertible deck lid ski rack. Strato-ease headrests. Speed warning unit. Portable hand spotlight. Special cast-aluminum wheels.

SPECIFICATIONS

1967 STING RAY POWER TEAMS

Engine Bore & Stroke	Horsepower & Torque at RPM	Carburetion & Induction System	Comp. Ratio	Cam & Lifters	Trans-missions	Axle Ratios	
						Standard	Positraction
STANDARD ENGINE							
327-cu.-in. V8	300 @ 5000	4-Barrel	10.0:1	General Performance	3-Speed (2.54:1 Low)	3.36:1	3.08:1 3.36:1
4.00 x 3.25 ins.	360 @ 3400	High-Flow Air Cleaner		Hydraulic	4-Speed (2.52:1 Low)	3.36:1	3.08:1 3.36:1
					Powerglide	3.36:1	3.36:1
EXTRA-COST OPTIONAL ENGINES							
327-cu.-in V8	350 @ 5800	4-Barrel	11.0:1	High Performance	4-Speed (2.52:1 Low)	3.36:1	3.36:1 3.55:1
4.00 x 3.25 ins.	360 @ 3600	High-Flow Air Cleaner		Hydraulic	4-Speed (2.20:1 Low)	3.70:1	3.70:1 4.11:1
427-cu.-in. V8	390 @ 5400	4-Barrel	10.25:1	High Performance	4-Speed (2.52:1 Low)	3.08:1*	3.36:1
4.251 x 3.76 ins.	460 @ 3600	High-Flow Air Cleaner		Hydraulic	4-Speed (2.20:1 low)	3.36:1*	3.08:1 3.55:1
					Powerglide	3.36:1*	3.70:1
427-cu.-in. V8	400 @ 5400	Triple 2-Barrel	10.25:1	High Performance	4-Speed (2.52:1 Low)	3.08:1*	3.36:1
4.251 x 3.76 ins.	400 @ 3600	High-Flow Air Cleaner		Hydraulic	4-Speed (2.20:1 Low)	3.36:1*	3.08:1 3.55:1 3.70:1
					Powerglide		
427-cu.-in. V8	435 @ 5800	Triple 2-Barrel	11.0:1	Special Performance	4-Speed (2.20:1 Low)	3.55:1*	3.36:1 3.70:1 4.11:1
4.251 x 3.76 ins.	460 @ 4000	High-Flow Air Cleaner		Mechanical			

*Available as Positraction only

Ten colors are offered for 1967: Tuxedo Black, Ermine White, Elkhart Blue, Lynndale Blue, Marina Blue, Goodwood Green, Marlboro Maroon, Rally Red, Silver Pearl, and Sunfire Yellow.

1967 brought a re-focus of Corvette promotional material to emphasize the luxury characteristics that are standard with this car. From the bright-metal-trimmed, foam-rubber padded, vinyl-covered bucket seats, to the safety-padded instrument panel, everything was "a devotee's delight". Special emphasis was placed on the subtle features, like the 999 mile trip odometer that had been standard in Corvette for years, the ubiquitous parking brake and headlight warning lights, and relocated (but functionally unchanged) control knobs.

In addition, there was the expected series of optional performance equipment including engine choices up to a new high of 435 horsepower (achieved by incorporating three two-barrel carburetors on last years biggest 427 cid engine), special front and rear-suspension, heavy-duty brakes, cast-aluminum wheels, etc., all of which adds up to one thing for 1967, "Luxury Car or a Sports Car . . . it's both".

1967 Corvette Sting Ray Sport Coupe

Mr. Cliff Stoffer, Oceanside, California

7 Sting Ray Convertible with removable Hardtop.

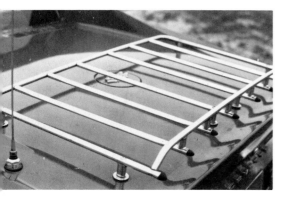

In addition to this optional rear deck luggage rack introduced in 1966, there is also an optional deck lid ski rack.

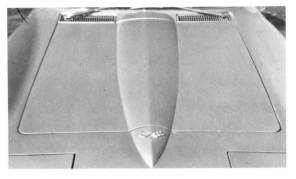

The standard engine, the 327 cid, is covered with the now familiar Corvette hood with the single long windsplit.

A new hood design, used exclusively in 1967, and differing from the 1966 style, is employed with the big 427 cid engines. The 427 insignia (upper right) appears on the sides of the dome.

For 1967, the standard wheels are fitted with wide chromed beauty rings and new small hub caps.

The 427 hoods are two-toned and striped as shown. The inner color choice is limited to either black or white, with a matching stripe.

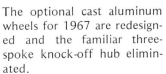

The optional cast aluminum wheels for 1967 are redesigned and the familiar three-spoke knock-off hub eliminated.

Although an obvious change appears at the fender vents (compare with page 230), a less noticible change is the deletion of the familiar crossed flag emblem above them.

A restyling of the rocker panel mouldings presents a smoother appearance in that area.

A smooth quarter panel in the Sport Coupes is unchanged from 1966 when the vent openings were eliminated.

In 1967, the power-operated, telescoping radio antenna is replaced, after only two years use, with a non-telescoping, single wire unit specially tuned for **maximum AM and FM reception.**

The familiar Corvette chamfered tail pipes protrude through the rear of the body and are well protected by wraparound bumpers.

New for 1967 is a wide rectangular back up lamp which utilizes two separate lenses. (left)

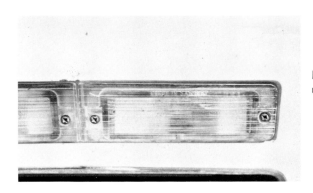

Although the Sting Ray Convertible rear deck does not have an access lid, the forward portion of the deck does open to provide access to the folded soft top storage area.

A new fuel filler cap appears again in 1967. This one, the first made of metal rather than plastic, has its center painted to match the body color.

With the addition to a separate back up lamp (previous page), there is a return to two red lensed tail lights on each side.

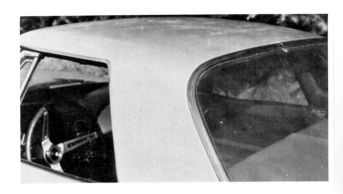

Standard for the Corvette Sting Ray Convertible is the folding soft top (left), in black, white, or new teal blue, *or* the removable hard top (above), although *both* may be optionally obtained. For the first time, the hard top could be ordered with an exterior black vinyl dress-up covering.

Tops are secured to the windshield frame with two chromed latches.

The interior of the removable hard top is upholstered with a sound deadening vinyl for excellent effect.

Both tops must be recessed at the bottom rear to clear the decorative windsplit.

Tops are secured to the sides of the cockpit w[ith] hex-headed bolts.

e inside non-glare rear view mirror, an
tion in 1966, is standard equipment for
67. With vinyl-edged shatter-resistant
ss, it is mounted on a breakaway sup-
rt for added safety.

Subtle details identify this as the 1967 interior. These would
include the pattern of the upholstery on the seats and the relocated inside door lock, now near the center of the door.

ats are upholstered in vinyl with leather
an option in black, red, bright blue,
rk blue, or saddle. All-vinyl interiors
clude black, red, bright blue, dark teal
ue, saddle, green, and white/black or
hite/bright blue.

New this year are latching seat
backs.

Controls for the incoming air vents have
been removed from their accustomed
place under the instrument panel astride
the steering column, and placed directly
on the sides of the console.

The appearance of the inside door lock is unchanged, but it has been moved forward near the center of the door.

Plastic knobs are introduced on both window cranks.

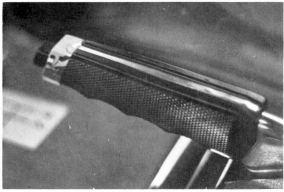

New this year is the console-mounted hand brake lever replacing the earlier T-handle suspended under the instrument panel. With a button-release at its tip, and tooled grips it *suggested* more excitement.

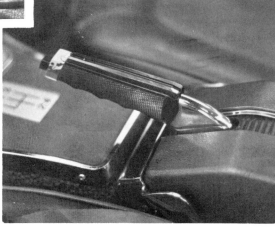

Mounted in the console are the air conditioning and the AM/FM pushbutton radio, both of which remain options.

The three spring steel spokes of the wood grained steering wheel recess the hub for safety. A telescoping steering column is available as an option.

The standard speedometer has not changed since 1965, but a new option appears this year (below).

The standard 300 hp 327 cid engine uses this tachometer which is red-lined at 5000 rpm. All other engines offered this year come equipped with the tachometer below.

A new adjustable audible speed warning is an option this year and accounts for the extra pointer on this speedometer.

The standard electric clock with the sweep second hand and 24 hour dial is continued this year.

The optional AM/FM push button radio is identical with the 1965 and 1966 model.

248

This unique Air Injector Reactor (A.I.R.) pump is an optional accessory which allegedly "pressurized the manifold to increase the volume of air fed to the cylinders", and was actually a California-required smog-reducing device.

alternator is mounted on the left of the engine block.

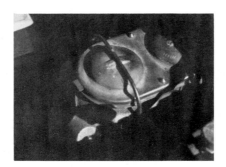

The brake master cylinder is mounted on the firewall.

tructions for filling are contain-
on the side of the coolant reser-
r.

Distributor shielding continues to be required with the non-metallic body.

1968 Corvette Sting Ray Coupe

Mr. Ramiro Contreras, Carlsbad, California

1968 saw a major change in the appearance of the Corvette ich was then only superficially refined in 1969. With the earance of a much longer car, it is interesting to note that wheelbase of 98'' has been unchanged since 1963. Among most innovative of the new features are the removable els in the roof of the coupe, its removable rear window, the new pop-up (rather than rotating) headlights. Other, obvious, new features include a 20 gallon plastic fuel tank ghing less than the conventional steel tank, and crankcase ne return lines on the bigger engines. Standard was still the) hp newly-named Turbo-Fire 327 cid engine, while per-mance options offered the big 427 cid (with a special hood) versions up to 435 horsepower. (In 1969 the 327 engine replaced with a new 350 cid version, but ratings were ntially unchanged).

1968 colors include Tuxedo Black, British Green, Inter-ional Blue, Polar White, Silverstone Silver, Rally Red, vette Bronze, Safari Yellow, Corovan Maroon, and Le s Blue. In 1969, the colors, which vary slightly, were amed for obvious effect: Can-Am White, Monza Red, Mans Blue, Fathom Green, Daytona Yellow, Cortez Silver, naco Orange, Burgundy, Riverside Gold, and Tuxedo Black.

The distinctive new lines of the rear end are part of an over-all appearance restyling.

9 Corvette Stingray Convertible   *Mr. Edward Imgrund, Escondido, California*

1968 Corvette Sting Ray Coupe

1969 Corvette Stingray Convertib

Standard hood for 1968-69 is similar to earlier hoods and has single long wind-split, but does not interchange. In 1969 the standard 327 cid Turbo-Fire engine was replaced with a Turbo-Fire 350 cid.

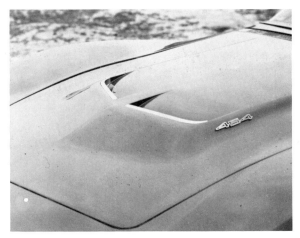

The optional larger 427 cid engine is supplied with this hood having two reversed scoops. Shown here on a 1971 model, the earlier models bear a 427 insignia.

Headlights pop up above the bumper rather than rotate as previously. An interesting item introduced in 1969 is a remotely controlled water jet to wash the lamps.

The grill has been widened and now extends beyond the parking light almost to the side of the fender.

In 1969, Corvette introduced the single-word "Stingray" and placed it in script above the four fender vents (above). 1968 models did not have this feature (left).

A new outside rear view mirror appears in 1968.

The windshield wipers are now concealed.

A vacuum operated solendoid (lower left) raises a section of the cowl, and the concealed windshield wipers go into action.

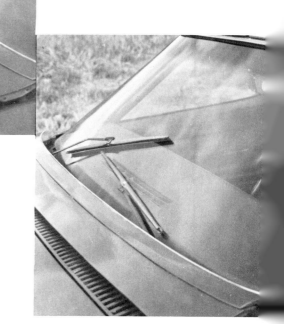

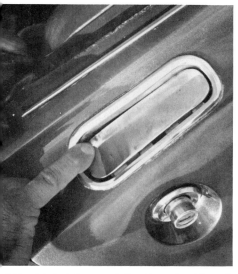

This combination button release door lock appears in 1968 only. For 1969, it is replaced by a one-purpose outside door lock.

968, this bright metal flap is spring-hinged offer a finger grip for leverage against the n-button outside door release below it. nged in 1969 to a full-mechanism release, push button release is then deleted.

A new non-collapsing, fixed height, antenna mounts at the rear.

The rear window of the Coupe is removable and may be stored with the roof panels. Behind the window is a vent for inside air when the cockpit is enclosed. The system, known as Astro Ventilation permits a controlled air flow even with the windows closed.

The roof panels of the Coupe may be unlatched and removed if desired.

With roof panels removed, the open framework of the Coupe resembles the letter, hence the popular name for the model, "T-Top".

Removed roof panels are stored and strapped in place in an area provided behind the seats.

A popular option is a vinyl covering applied to the movable hard top for a Convertible. Only available black, it features chromed metal covers at the rear

Receptacles are provided in the frame for latching the roof panels.

e 1968 Corvette has back up lights placed
ow the rear bumper in a protected location.
e lens, manufactured by the Guide division of
is similar to that used in 1967 (page 242),
slightly different inside, it bears a new num-

For 1969, the back up light is once again placed in the
inner pair of tail lights and the separate lamp eliminated.
The "keylock" above the name at the right of the picture
is for a built-in security alarm system, a new option this
year.

The Corvette name is lettered across the rear of
the car.

Side marker lights that
illuminate with the
headlights are new stan-
dard equipment starting
in 1968.

This gas filler cap with raised flags is
used from 1968 on.

Wide doors are curved at their rear end to flare into body.

For 1968, the standard vinyl interiors are available in Tobacco, red, black, medium blue, dark blue, dark orange and gunmetal. Genuine leather interiors include black, red, medium blue, dark orange, or tobacco.

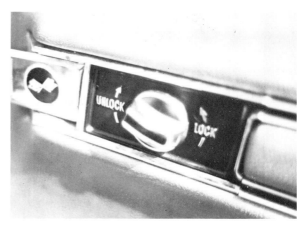

Many subtle luxury features are provided including the labeling of the functions of the inside door lock knob and the use of the Corvette crossed flags on the inside door handle seen to the left of the photo.

The optional telescoping steering column is locked by this lever at its hub.

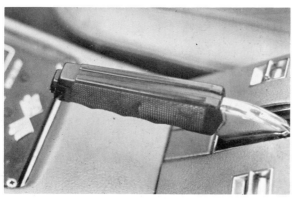

Optional power windows are controlled by these switches astride the parking brake handle on the console.

1968 interior

A new 7000 rpm tachometer, like the speedometer, places the numbers outside of the calibrated circle.

deeply recessed 160 mph speedometer now ludes an odometer built into its face. The nter set at 80 mph is part of the optional ed warning system which buzzes at a pre-set ed.

An impressive new instrument cluster is installed at the upper center console. Dials are not identical with earlier units as decorative arcs have been added. The optional AM/FM pushbutton radio is joined by an addtional option, that of an FM multiplex stereo system.

Seat belts are standard, and also shoulder belts in the Coupe.

The marker, parking, and tail lights may be flashed at will by a hazard warning feature controlled by a switch below the steering wheel.

1968 interior shown

Indicators on the console beneath the radio indicate operation of lights.

Air Conditioning, AM/FM Radio, and Hydra-Matic automatic transmission are all options. The ignition lock (upper left) has a new audible buzzer alarm to remind drivers to remove keys when leaving car.

Additional indicators below the shift lever monitor the rear lights. A new optional transmission with full automatic *or* manual shifting is introduced. With a straight line shift pattern, it replaces the Powerglide name with new Turbo Hydra-Matic.

To the left of the built-in ashtray lighter are new thumb-wheel cont for the heater and optional air co tioner.

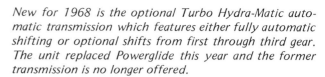

New for 1968 is the optional Turbo Hydra-Matic automatic transmission which features either fully automatic shifting or optional shifts from first through third gear. The unit replaced Powerglide this year and the former transmission is no longer offered.

Hinged at the front, Corvette's hood opens from the rear for engine service.

The metal box is distributor shielding, still required to eliminate interference. In the foreground is the vacuum piston which opens the cowl over the concealed windshield wipers.

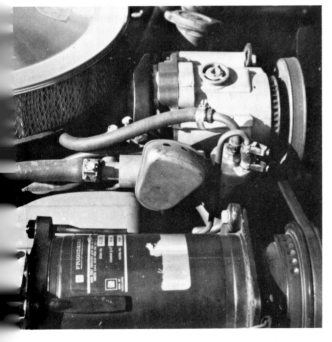

n the left side of the engine is a belt-driven alternator; e unit on the right is an optional air conditioning comessor.

All Corvette engines from 1968 on are equipped with Air Injection Reactor equipment to control exhaust emissions, but bigger and bigger engines have packed Corvette's engine compartment leaving little room for more growth.

1970-71-72

1970 Stingray Coupe

1971 Stingray Coupe

For 1970-71-72, Corvette again offered two models, the Stingray Coupe and the Stingray Convertible. Greatly resembling the 1968-69 model, they are within themselves so similar as to defy easy identification.

1972 Stingray Coupe

The removable panels of the Stingray Coupe, a popular feature, are retained in this series.

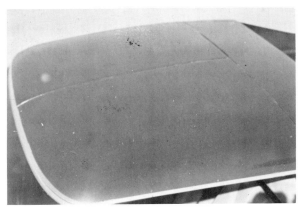

Starting in 1970, a new engine, the Turbo-Jet 454 replaces the earlier 427 options with a maximum performance version rated at 460 horsepower! (two years later, in 1972, emission controls and a different method of rating reduced this rating to 270 hp) but the standard 300 hp Turbo-Fire 350 engine remained unchanged (by 1972, its rating was down to 200 hp).

The Tubo-Fire 350 engine is placed under this hood which is standard for the series.

The hood for the big Tubo-Jet 454 engine has reversed scoops for better cooling.

op-up headlights and a wide fender-to-fender bumper ontinue as does the crossed flag insignia.

A new egg-crate grill with distinctive parking lights replaces the earlier style (page 253).

The rocker panel moulding, common for all three years, is shaped to emphasize the lines of the fender.

A feature last seen in 1972 is the wide chrome bumper at the front of the car.

All three years of this series share the grill pattern on the fender vent, and the Stingray insignia above it.

The exhaust grill of the Astro-Vent air flow system is continued on both Coupe and Convertible on which it is placed somewhat more to the rear.

Such a strong similarity exists that for 1970 a 1971, the sales catalogs, although differing in te share the same illustrations!

The Anti-theft alarm system is reset by the ignition key at a lock at the rear. Options in 1970 and 1971, the system became standard equipment in 1972.

The square exhaust pipe introduced in 1970 continues through 1973 model.

Back up lights are built in and are standard equipment.

These marker lights at the corners of the car are illuminated with the headlights.

1970 Interior shown

The Coupe is equipped with a shoulder belt which for convenience passes through the high-backed seat.

1970 Interiors are done in black, saddle, dark brown, blue, red, or dark green vinyl, or black or saddle genuine leather. 1971 colors were the same except for the saddle and dark brown vinyl which were combined to offer "dark saddle"

A new map storage compartment has been added at the right, but the deeply recessed instruments of the preceding series are repeated.

The center console has become truly a control center with monitoring instruments and warning lights plus an optional AM/FM pushbutton radio *or* an AM/FM multiplex stereo radio.

An identification data plate, placed at the bottom rear of the control console, defines the engine choice. This is for the standard engine.

1973 Corvette Stingray Coupe   *Mrs. Lu Ann Holden, Oceanside, California*

1974 Corvette Stingray Coupe   *Mr. Ken Wexleberger, Oceanside, Califor[n]*

e crossed flags of past
rs have been replaced with
se medallions on this ser-
For 1973 and 1974, the
blem bore the Company
ne (above), in 1975, this
s deleted (right).

'75 Corvette Stingray Coupe

Courtesy Wesseloh Chevrolet, Oceanside, California

1973-74-75

The chrome bumper trim bar of past years has been deleted starting in 1973, and the entire nose section is now the bumper.

A new hood is introduced which serves all engines in this series.

The pop-up headlights are continued unchanged.

All cars in this series have a characteris single-vent in the fenders surmounted the Stingray emblem.

Starting in 1973, the entire nose section is actually a steel-supported urethane bumper which gains help in 1975 (below) from the addition of resilent honeycomb blocks to cushion minor impact.

The rear edge of the hood is curved upward to conceal the windshield wipers beneath.

A new die cast aluminum grill turing horizontal lines appears this series.

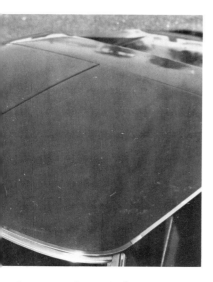

e Coupe roof panels (and rear win-
w) are again removable.

Panels are individually removable and if desired, either may be left in place.

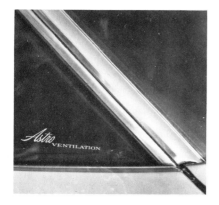

The Astro ventilation system permits cockpit air to be exhausted through controlled vent at the rear even with the windows rolled up.

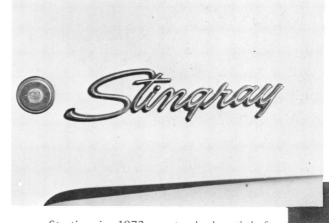

Starting in 1973, a standard anti-theft alarm system control has been added on the left front fender just ahead of the Stingray emblem.

271

1973

The wraparound bumper and the square exhaust pipe i strongly reminiscent of the 1972 model (page 265)

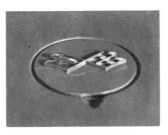

The gas filler lid again has the crossed flags motif.

The bumper extends cleanly around the side and to the forward edge of the marker light.

1974

For this series a one-piece (non-lowering) antenna is standard with either optional radio.

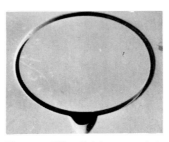

The gas filler lid is now plain with no emblem.

The rear section now has become the bump with the deletion of the former external wra around. Under a resilient urethane fairing the is a steel framework for protection.

The exhaust vent for the Astro-ventilation system is directly behind the rear window. On the Convertible, it is located further to the rear to allow for the hatch cover for the folding soft top.

...o frame-mounted hydraulic cylinders support an ...minum bumper under a urethane cover to provide ...r bumper protection.

A new fuel filler lid appears in 1975 featuring, in addition to a matching hood ornament, a warning regarding the necessary fuel.

...e rear lights have a red, or a frosted center, depending on whether they are ...ployed as the back up lights (inner pair).

A resilient honeycomb plastic block is added at the rear corners to aid in absorbing minor impacts. Like the urethane cover itself, they are self-restoring.

First offered in 1969, the Tilt-
Telescoping steering wheel permits
an individual adjustment from
seven tilt positions and six inches
of travel. It is controlled by the
lever under the directional signal
lever.

The 1975 interior is shown here.

Due to its unusual affinity for over-size tires and magnesium wheels, Corvette is not infrequently observed with "incorrect" wheels. An owner's preference in this regard must be respected, but for the reader to whom "authentic" is a respectable condition to which he aspires, we present an illustration of the appropriate wheel covers for each model year.

WHEEL COVERS

1954-55

Perhaps the most attractive, certainly the most colorful, the serrations of the 1954-55 covers were decorated in bright red paint.

1956-57-58

Used for three years, the 1956-58 covers have a distinctive two-bar spinner at their hub.

1959-62

...ically similar to the 1956-58 style, the
...59-62 has slots added at its perimeter,
... is the most common cover due to
...four years of use.

1963

Early in the model year, the covers were
furnished with a brushed finish at the
inner ring.

...ring the 1963 model year, the brushed
...sh, an extra manufacturing operation,
... discontinued and the covers furnished
...lusively in bright metal.

WHEEL COVERS

1964

A less elaborate cover was furnished with the 1964 model. Although retaining the three-bar "spinner" of 1963, the stamping at the hub changed and the face plate is far simpler.

Early in the model year, a brushed finish was furnished, but this was quickly abandoned.

1965

Six wedge-shaped slots grace the covers in 1965, and the hub of the familiar spinner now is black.

1966

Returning to a more elaborate style, the 1966 cover has five larger wedge-shaped slots opening onto a simulated brake drum.

Optional cast aluminum knock-off hub wheels with 6" rims were first offered for the 1963 model. They continued to be available through 1967 although there are some differences among them.

In 1963 and early 1964, the center was chromed but no paint appeared between the spokes. During 1964, the black paint there improved the appearance.

Initially furnished in 1963 with two-ear knock-off spinners, these were almost immediately changed to three-ear to facilitate the use of the lead hammer needed to tighten them.

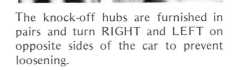

The knock-off hubs are furnished in pairs and turn RIGHT and LEFT on opposite sides of the car to prevent loosening.

The 1967 cast aluminum wheel eliminated the knock-off flanged spinner and returned to a conventional bolt-on style. The five lug nuts are reached by removing the center cap.

he chromed center flange persisted through 965, but by 1966 was being painted black.

WHEEL COVERS

1967

The standard covers for 1967 include a small hub cap and a wide outer beauty ring. The wheels are slotted and can be seen between the two dress-up items.

Hubs are stamped with identifying information. The disc brakes referred to became standard at all four wheels in 1965.

The wide outer beauty ring fits over the wheel flange.

First available in 1967 with a "bow tie" insignia at its hub, the optional dress-up full wheel cover is an infrequently seen accessory. From 1968 to 1975 it is "correct" as an alternative to the standard wheel cover below.

Similar in effect to the earlier style, the 1968-75 standard wheel cover is again a small hub cap plus an outer beauty ring. The hub cap has been changed and now has an attractive pattern of serrations behind its lettered hub.

Although these attractive cast aluminum wheels, (15 x 8.00), were offered in 1973 and 1974, they were never readily available and were discontinued in early 1975, then reintroduced as an available option on the 1976 models.

Special Trim Items

1954-55 Front Emblem

1956-57 Front Emblem

1958 Front and Rear Emblem. It is also used on 1961 rear and 1962 rear with black backing plate. Originally lettered in gold, the replacements are now done in silver.

1961 Front Emblem

1962 Front Emblem

1963-64 Front Emblem

1965-66 Front Emblem

1967 Front Emblem

1968-72 Front Emblem

1973-74 Front Emblem

1975 Front Emblem

This 1957 Fuel Injection trim strip was used in three places on the car. Both fenders and the rear deck lid all were so decorated, the only year it appeared at the rear.

1958-61 Fuel Injection trim strip

1962 Fuel Injection trim strip

1963-64 Fuel Injection trim strip

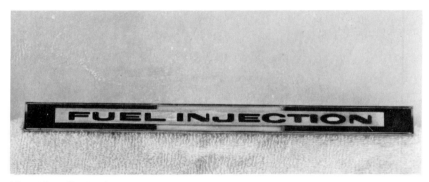

The 1965 Fuel Injection trim strip is unique to that year. Fuel Injection was discontinued in mid-year with the introduction of the big block Turbo-Jet 396.

Fuel Filler Doors

1963

1964

1965

1966

The 1967 was the first all-metal one. Its background is painted to match the body color.

1974

1968-73

1975

SPECIAL TRIM ITEMS

1958-60 (also on 1957 Fuel Injected cars)

Fender Side Trim emblems

1961

1962-66

1962-63 on left; 1963-66 on right. Note difference in thickness (above).

1966 only

Mid-1965 only
(big block engine)

This emblem is placed on the *hood* of the cars so equipped in 1967-68-69.

1963-65 Rear Deck Trim

1966-67 Rear Deck Trim

1969-75 Front Fender Trim

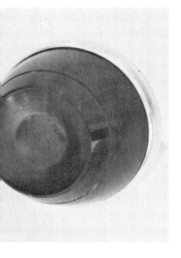

954-55 Tail Light Assembly

1956-57 lens (right), shown with the smaller 1961-67 Tail Light lens.

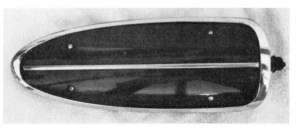

1958-60 Tail Light Assembly

1954-55 Headlight

1956-57 Headlight

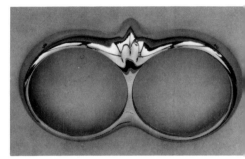

1958-59-60 Headlight

1961-62

1963-67

1968-75

Miniatures

"Promotional Models" of the car are generally those distributed by the Factory or the Dealers and often have specially detailed undersides or running gear. "Kits" are just that, commercially available assembly kits, generally of some fairly accurate detail, and assembled by the buyer. Also available at times are assembled versions, often with friction motors, and also referred to as "models". Accordingly, we here display versions of the Corvette scaled down and referred to generally as "Miniatures".

The collection of these Miniatures is a fast-growing hobby, and we are pleased that we have been able to isolate a full run of the miniatures on a year-by-year basis.

(left to right) 1963 Corvette, AMT 1/32 scale; 1964 Ideal Motoriffic; 1963 die cast by Corgi; 1963 Aurora (Match Box Series); front center: 1965 Hard Top by Sabra; 1965 Sport Coupe by Renwall

Early 1954 friction motor model by PMC. Note early style wheels.

Late 1954 friction motor model, PMC with white-wall tires and silver wheel covers.

The 1955 model by PMC has Chevrolet-style wheel covers.

MINIATURES

1956 MPC (Model Plastic Corp.) kit. A soft top was available with kit.

1956 kit with Hard Top

Two 1956 kits

1957 MPC kit

In 1957 some kits were furnished wi miniature license plates.

1958 SMP (Scale Model Products) kits show a bit better detail and are more authentic.

8 PMC kit. This was available in both a hard top model also a Soft top version. Hood Louvers are quite pronced.

For the first time, PMC included Corvette-style wheel covers on their 1959 Convertible and Hard Top friction motored models.

1959 SMP friction motor model. This was also available in kit form.

1959 SMP kit. A hard top was also available.

MINIATURES

Revelle factory-built model with driver, opening hood, and fully detailed engine.

1960 SMP friction motor model

1960 SMP kit. This was the first year for the opening hood.

1962 SMP Promotional Model. Also available in kit form and as a friction motor model. Corvette's Promotional Models first became available starting in 1958.

1961 SMP friction motor model (also available as a kit). This was the first year for a front wheel drive friction motor.

1963 Sting Ray Coupe Promotional Model by AMT. This was their first Corvette model.

1963 Sting Ray Convertible by AMT. Available in kit form only, it was not furnished with a hard top. The 1963 version was the only one to have revolving headlights.

1963 Sting Ray Convertible (with a 1965 hard top). No hard tops were furnished with the 1963-64 kits but they may be retrofitted easily. Note excellent headlight detail.

1964 Promotional Model by AMT. Also available in kit form.

1964 Sting Ray Convertible by AMT. Available both as a Promotional Model and also as a kit.

1965 AMT kit model with optional hard top. 1965 was the first year that the top was available.

1965 Sting Ray Coupe by AMT. This is a Promotional Model, but a kit was also offered.

1965 Sting Ray Convertible Promotional Model by AMT. (also available as a kit.)

1966 Sting Ray Coupe by AMT. This is the Promotional Model, and a kit was also available.

1966 Sting Ray Convertible Promotional Model by AMT. Also available as a kit, the kit included an optional Hard Top.

1966 Sting Ray Sport Coupe by MPC (Model Plastic Corp.). Available in kit form only, it came equipped with optional 427 hood (shown), side exhaust pipes, and knock-off wheels.

1967 Sting Ray Coupe by AMT. This as a Promotional Model and was equipped with the stock 327 hood. Also available as a kit, the kit came with the 427 hood (left).

The 1967 Convertibles by AMT differed in similar fashion to the Coupes. The Promotional Model (left) has the 427 hood; the kit (right) has the standard 327 type hood.

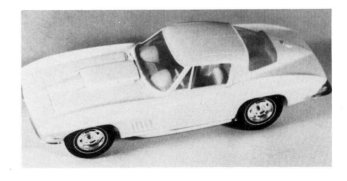

1967 Sting Ray Coupe kit by AMT.

MINIATURES

1968 Sting Ray Coupe by MPC. Available in kit form only, as no Promotional Models were available in 1968.

1968 Sting Ray Convertible by MPC. This is a promotional Model and was also available as a kit.

For 1968, AMT had a kit only. Assembled as either a Hard Top or open Convertible, it is not as detailed as the MPC version.

The 1969 Stingray Convertible by AMT. This is a promotional model, a kit was also available.

1969 Corvettes by AMT were available both as Promotional Models and also as kits.

1969 Coupe by AMT. Available both as Promotional Model and as kit.

1969 MPC "Dyno-Racer". This is a Promotional Model body on a die cast chassis equipped with "Hot Wheels". It was available assembled and with track on which it would run.

296

1970 AMT Convertible promotional Model. Also available in kit form.

1970 Promotional Model by AMT. Also available as a kit. Although by now the rear fenders on the Corvette are flared, the miniatures lacked that feature.

1971 MPC Promotional model.

1971 MPC Convertible. Available in kit only.

1972 Coupe by MPC. A Promotional Model, it is also available as a kit.

1972 Convertible by MPC. Available in kit only.

MINIATURES

1973 Coupe by MPC. Available both as Promotional and as Kit Models.

1973 Convertible by MPC. From 1971 on, the Convertibles were available in kit form only.

1974 Coupe by MPC. A Promotional Model, it is also available in kit form.

1974 Convertible (kit form only) by MPC

1975 Coupe by MPC, available as both Promotional Model and as a kit.

1975 Convertible by MPC, available in kit form on

1954-55 Banthrico
Only 1000 of these were made, each with its own serial number. Made of pot metal they were available in red, white, or blue only. They were manufactured in 1974 and are very well detailed.

The Astro-Vette by MPC, available in kit form only, has fender skirts and cowl vents and is patterned on a full-size experimental version of the Corvette.

A similar effort is this Mako Shark by MPC, a miniature of an early Corvette "dream car" effort.

The Astro-1 by AMT commemorated still another "dream car" prepared by Corvette.

A 1/20th scale gasoline engine driven miniature by Cox was ma[de] for only three model years 1964-65-67 (1965 model show[n]). Notice the size compared with the conventional 1/24 sc[ale] miniature on the left.

1968 1/20th scale model by MPC (availab[le] through 1975 model year) has optional po[p] up headlights and removable top as well [as] a fully detailed engine compartment.

The largest of them all, the 1/8th scale by Monogram is a 1965 Sting Ray Coupe almost 22" long over all, and features opening hood, revolving head lights, and a fully detailed interior and undercarriage.

1955 Corvette by Hubley. About 13" long over all, it has a six cylinder engine under an opening hood. Also has opening rear deck and while quite well detailed, curiously shows the spare tire mounted *above* the floor in the luggage compartment. The front wheels are steerable.

Ideal Toy Company's 1954 model. About 16" long, the hood and rear lid both open. This includes jeweled tail lights among its many excellent trim features.

ft rear: Corvette Rondine Pinin Farina (Politoys, Italy); right rear: Sting Ray by Corgi (note side pipes, mag wheels; Front left to ht: 68 Sting Ray Coupe by Lindberg; 69 Coupe by Playard (Hong Kong); 1955 Convertible by Hubley; Mako Shark by Aurora; and 69 Sting Ray Coupe by AMT.

The Unreal Corvette

With perhaps the exceptions only of the Model T Ford and the Volkswagen, no car other than Corvette has so adapted itself to the imaginations of its owners. Aside from the symbolism that ownership of a Corvette may provide, there is a special desire apparent in many owners to customize their cars and thus provide one that is just a little different than all others.

Few of the total Corvettes are modified for the purpose of providing better "racing" characteristics. Rather, most seem to have been customized for reasons ranging from whimsy to envy with a strong flavoring of plain innovation.

No rules apply in this game; owners do to their cars what they will, and if not satisfied with the results, hack a little more off or glass a little more on. Putty and paint cover former mounting holes; the hoods and wheel wells are easily adapted to fiber glass shrouds; wide rear wheels (for "better traction") are often mated with small front wheels (for "better steering"); bumpers are removed, and hoods interchanged. Underneath it all lies Corvette, like a patient elderly man allowing children of another generation to enjoy their play with him, and knowing all the while that when they tire of their game, he is still unchanged.

With bumpers removed, wide wheels added, and modifications made to a stock 67 hood, this 1966 Sting Ray Convertible with Removable Hard Top is deceptively quiet. Equipped with a 1970 454 cid engine rated at 460 horsepower, and a straight-line shifter for its 4-speed heavy duty transmission, it is a strong competitor in acceleration trials.

A mild customizing of a stock 1963 Sting Ray Sport Coupe adds side exhaust pipes (first available in 1965), and flared fenders to cover wider-than-stock tires on mag wheels.

One of the earliest "customizing" efforts was this experimental Corvette shown in a 1957 factory folder. Perhaps showing the way to future tinkerers, the car was greatly modified. A light-weight magnesium alloy body formed over a tubular frame, low plastic windscreens at front and sides, large cooling side vents and sharply tapered rear deck were all features that were emphasized by the addition of a removable canopy. The car was considered purely experimental and was never placed in production.

THE UNREAL CORVETTE

A 1967 454 cid engine and hood are mated to a 1958 Corvette.

Hood latching pins are an infrequent, but imaginative custom item. Hardly necessary, since the Corvette hood is hinged at the front, they add a "sporty" touch.

In addition to the hood latching pins, this hood has been fitted with an imaginative custom bubble.

For further custom effect, the front trim of the hood scoop is omitted and the mounting holes sealed.

Under the hood custom valve covers and a high rise manifold combine for special effect.

Perhaps the ultimate indignity is the practice of "relieving" the hood when non-stock engine parts "just don't fit".

Super-bright driving lights, mounted below the grill require the relocation of the front license plate (and the elimination of the center bumper section).

Several types of wire wheels are used by customizers. Perhaps because of cost, they lack the popularity of the mag wheels. This set has shorter spokes, set deep into the wheel rim.

This set of custom wire wheels has longer spokes fitted into a larger inside diameter rim.

THE UNREAL CORVETTE

Light weight magnesium alloy or cast aluminum wheels are probably the most popular single item of custom nature. They are available in a variety of shapes and width depending upon the manufacturer.

Fiber-glass "flares" can be added to stock wheel housing to cover wider tires and wheels.

The front fender wheel opening h been customized to provide a "d ferent" look.

306

...ghly popular in California, a third pair of rear lights can ...ily be added to the 1963-67 Corvettes.

Paint and striping is a matter of personal preference. Efforts can range from the simple embellishment shown here to an unimaginably wild set of stars and stripes.

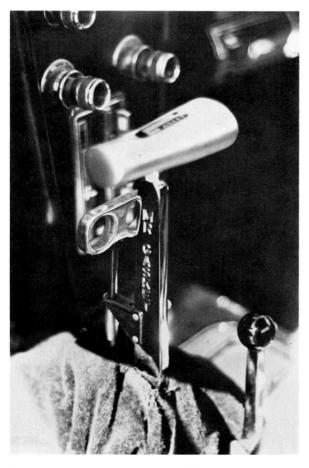

Quick-reaction transmission shifters offer special linkages to improve transmission gear shift times. This one, by incorporating a mechanical interlock (below handle) to block 1st and 2nd range, allows shifting in a straight line back-and-forth pattern through all four ranges. Reverse is reached with the aid of the short black-knobbed handle behind it.

An enterprising, and cautious, owner has added an anti-theft alarm system to his 1962 Corvette by concealing the lock in his fender ornament.

Engines

1954 Blue Flame Six
During 1954 the painted valve
cover was replaced with a chromed
one. In 1955 the engine was
slightly modified and given
12 volt accessories.

1955 265 cubic inch V-8 Engine.
Photo is of passenger car version.

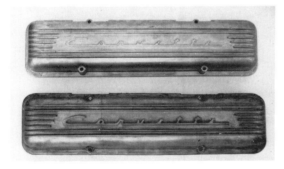

(top) 1956-59 "staggered hole" valve covers;
used on high-performance engines only. Below
it is the 1960-67 "straight-hole" performance
engine valve covers. Standard was a stamped
steel cover.

1957 283 cid V-8 with Ramjet Fuel Injection

1957 283 cubic inch displacement standard V-8 engine

photographs courtesy of Chevrolet Motor Divis

308

962-68 327 cid V-8 engine. Passenger car version shown.

1966-69 Turbo-Jet 427 cid V-8 Chevrolet engine

Cut away photograph of a 1965 396 cid Turbo-Jet V-8 Corvette engine

1969 Corvette Special High Performance 427 cid engine with Aluminum Block, Cylinder Heads, Intake Maniford. Rated at 430 horsepower at 5200 rpm (option # RPO ZL-1)

1969-1975 basic Corvette engine; Turbo-Fire 350 V-8 engine.

1970-74 High Performance optional
Turbo-Jet 454 V-8 engine

Appendix

1954-55 data plate is placed just below the windshield on the left cowl dog-leg.

In 1961 and 1962, the plate is found on the steering column, under the hood.

For 1956-1960, the data plate appears on the left door pillar.

For 1963-67, the data plate, now bearing additional information, is located on the firewall under the glove box door.

Starting in 1968, the serial number is imbedded in the left side of the dashboard where it can be viewed from outside.

CORVETTE PRODUCTION BY MODEL YEAR

YEAR	PRODUCTION	YEAR	PRODUCTIO
1953	300	1964	22,229
1954	3,640	1965	23,564
1955	700	1966	27,720
1956	3,467	1967	22,940
1957	6,339	1968	28,566
1958	9,168	1969	38,762
1959	9,437	1970	17,316
1960	10,261	1971	21,801
1961	10,939	1972	27,004
1962	14,531	1973	38,464
1963	21,513	1974	37,502

Production figures courtesy of Mr. J. P. Pike, Assistant Manager, Merchandisin Passenger Cars, Chevrolet Motor Division

GENERAL SPECIFICATIONS

Year	Engine	Carburetor	Bore and Stroke	Piston Displacement, Cubic Inches	Compression Ratio	Maximum Brake H.P. @ R.P.M.	Maximum Torque Lbs. Ft. @ R.P.M.	Normal Oil Pressure Pounds
1953–55	150 Horsepower............6-235	1 Barrel	3.5625 x 3.94	235	8.00	150 @ 4200	223 @ 2400	35
1955	195 Horsepower...........V8-265	2 Barrel	3.750 x 3.00	265	8.00	195 @ 5000	260 @ 3000	35
1956	210 Horsepower...........V8-265	4 Barrel	3.750 x 3.00	265	9.25	210 @ 5200	270 @ 3200	35
	225 Horsepower...........V8-265	Two 4 Bar.	3.750 x 3.00	265	9.25	225 @ 5200	270 @ 3600	35
1957–59	230 Horsepower...........V8-283	4 Barrel	3.875 x 3.00	283	9.50	230 @ 4800	300 @ 3000	35
	245 Horsepower...........V8-283	Two 4 Bar.	3.875 x 3.00	283	9.50	245 @ 5000	300 @ 3800	35
	250 Horsepower...........V8-283	Fuel Inj.	3.875 x 3.00	283	9.50	250 @ 5000	305 @ 3800	35
	270 Horsepower...........V8-283	Two 4 Bar.	3.875 x 3.00	283	10.50	270 @ 6000	285 @ 4200	35
	290 Horsepower...........V8-283	Fuel Inj.	3.875 x 3.00	283	10.50	290 @ 6200	290 @ 4400	35
1960–61	230 Horsepower...........V8-283	4 Barrel	3.875 x 3.00	283	9.50	230 @ 4800	300 @ 3000	45
	245 Horsepower...........V8-283	Two 4 Bar.	3.875 x 3.00	283	9.50	245 @ 5000	300 @ 3800	45
	275 Horsepower...........V8-283	Fuel Inj.	3.875 x 3.00	283	11.00	275 @ 5200		45
	270 Horsepower...........V8-283	Two 4 Bar	3.875 x 3.00	283	9.50	270 @ 6000	285 @ 4200	45
	315 Horsepower...........V8-283	Fuel Inj.	3.875 x 3.00	283	11.00	315 @ 6200		45
1962	250 Horsepower...........V8-327	4 Barrel	4.0000 x 3.25	327	10.50	250 @ 4400	350 @ 2800	45
	300 Horsepower...........V8-327	4 Barrel	4.0000 x 3.25	327	10.50	300 @ 5000	360 @ 3200	45
	340 Horsepower (Spec. Cam)..V8-327	4 Barrel	4.0000 x 3.25	327	11.25	340 @ 6000	344 @ 4000	45
	360 Horsepower (Spec. Cam)..V8-327	Fuel Inj.	4.0000 x 3.25	327	11.25	360 @ 6000	352 @ 4000	45
1963	250 Horsepower...........V8-327	4 Barrel	4.001 x 3.25	327	10.50	250 @ 4400	350 @ 2800	45
	300 Horsepower...........V8-327	4 Barrel	4.001 x 3.25	327	10.50	300 @ 5000	360 @ 3200	45
	340 Horsepower...........V8-327	4 Barrel	4.001 x 3.25	327	11.25	340 @ 6000	344 @ 4000	45
	360 Horsepower...........V8-327	Fuel Inj.	4.001 x 3.25	327	11.25	360 @ 6000	352 @ 4000	45
1964	250 Horsepower...........V8-327	4 Barrel	4.0010 x 3.25	327	10.50	250 @ 4400	350 @ 2800	40
	300 Horsepower...........V8-327	4 Barrel	4.0010 x 3.25	327	10.50	300 @ 5000	360 @ 3200	40
	365 Horsepower...........V8-327	4 Barrel	4.0010 x 3.25	327	11.00	365 @ 6200	350 @ 4000	40
	375 Horsepower...........V8-327	Fuel Inj.	4.0010 x 3.25	327	11.00	375 @ 6200	350 @ 4600	40
1965	250 Horsepower...........V8-327	4 Barrel	4.001 x 3.25	327	10.50	250 @ 4400	350 @ 2800	40
	300 Horsepower...........V8-327	4 Barrel	4.001 x 3.25	327	10.50	300 @ 5000	360 @ 3200	40
	350 Horsepower...........V8-327	4 Barrel	4.001 x 3.25	327	11.00	350 @ 5800	360 @ 3600	40
	365 Horsepower...........V8-327	4 Barrel	4.001 x 3.25	327	11.00	365 @ 6200	350 @ 4000	40
	375 Horsepower...........V8-327	Fuel Inj.	4.001 x 3.25	327	11.00	375 @ 6200	350 @ 4600	40
1966	300 Horsepower...........V8-327	4 Barrel	4.001 x 3.25	327	10.5	300 @ 5000	360 @ 3400	30–45
	325 Horsepower...........V8-396	4 Barrel	4.094 x 3.76	396	10.25	325 @ 4800	410 @ 3200	50–75
	350 Horsepower...........V8-327	4 Barrel	4.001 x 3.25	327	11.0	350 @ 5800	360 @ 3600	30–45
	360 Horsepower...........V8-396	4 Barrel	4.094 x 3.76	396	10.25	360 @ 5200	420 @ 3600	50–75
	390 Horsepower...........V8-427	4 Barrel	4.251 x 3.76	427	10.25	390 @ 5200	470 @ 3600	50–75
	425 Horsepower...........V8-427	4 Barrel	4.251 x 3.76	427	11.0	425 @ 5600	460 @ 4000	50–75
1967	300 Horsepower...........V8-327	4 Barrel	4.001 x 3.25	327	10.00	300 @ 5000	360 @ 3400	30–45
	350 Horsepower...........V8-327	4 Barrel	4.001 x 3.25	327	11.00	350 @ 5800	360 @ 3600	30–45
	390 Horsepower...........V8-427	4 Barrel	4.251 x 3.76	427	10.25	390 @ 5400	460 @ 3600	30–35
	400 Horsepower...........V8-427	3 Carbs.	4.251 x 3.76	427	10.25	400 @ 5400	460 @ 3600	30–35
	425 Horsepower...........V8-427	4 Barrel	4.251 x 3.76	427	N.A.	N.A.	N.A.	30–35
	435 Horsepower...........V8-427	3 Carbs.	4.251 x 3.76	427	11.00	435 @ 5800	460 @ 4000	30–35

Year	Engine	Carburetor	Bore and Stroke	Piston Displacement, Cubic Inches	Compression Ratio	Maximum Brake H.P. @ R.P.M.	Maximum Torque Lbs. Ft. @ R.P.M.	Normal Oil Pressure Pounds
1968	300 Horsepower..........V8-327	4 Barrel	4.001 x 3.25	327	10.00	300 @ 5000	360 @ 3400	30–45
	350 Horsepower..........V8-396	4 Barrel	4.094 x 3.76	396	10.25	350 @ 5200	415 @ 3400	30–35
	390 Horsepower..........V8-427	4 Barrel	4.251 x 3.76	427	10.25	390 @ 5400	460 @ 3600	30–35
	400 Horsepower..........V8-427	3 Carbs.	4.251 x 3.76	427	10.25	400 @ 5400	460 @ 3600	30–35
	435 Horsepower..........V8-427	3 Carbs.	4.251 x 3.76	427	11.00	435 @ 5800	460 @ 4000	30–35
1969	300 Horsepower..........V8-350	4 Barrel	4.001 x 3.48	350	10.25	300 @ 4800	380 @ 3200	30–45
	350 Horsepower..........V8-350	4 Barrel	4.001 x 3.48	350	11.00	350 @ 5600	380 @ 3600	30–45
	390 Horsepower..........V8-427	4 Barrel	4.251 x 3.76	427	10.25	390 @ 5400	460 @ 3600	30–35
	400 Horsepower..........V8-427	4 Barrel	4.251 x 3.76	427	10.25	400 @ 5400	460 @ 3600	30–35
	425 Horsepower..........V8-427	4 Barrel	4.251 x 3.76	427	11.00	425 @ 5600	460 @ 4000	30–35
	430 Horsepower..........V8-427	4 Barrel	4.251 x 3.76	427	12.00	430 @ 5200	450 @ 4400	30–35
	435 Horsepower..........V8-427	3 Carbs.	4.251 x 3.76	427	11.00	435 @ 5800	460 @ 4000	30–35
1970	300 Horsepower..........V8-350	4 Barrel	4.001 x 3.48	350	10.25	300 @ 4800	380 @ 3200	30–45
	350 Horsepower..........V8-350	4 Barrel	4.001 x 3.48	350	11.00	350 @ 5600	380 @ 3600	30–45
	370 Horsepower..........V8-350	4 Barrel	4.001 x 3.48	350	11.00	370 @ 6000	380 @ 4000	30–45
	390 Horsepower..........V8-454	4 Barrel	4.251 x 4.00	454	10.25	390 @ 4800	500 @ 3400	
	460 Horsepower..........V8-454	4 Barrel	4.251 x 4.00	454	11.25	460 @ 5600	490 @ 3000	
1971	270 Horsepower..........V8-350	4 Barrel	4.00 x 3.48	350	8.50	270 @ 4800	360 @ 3200	
	330 Horsepower..........V8-350	4 Barrel	4.00 x 3.48	350	9.0	330 @ 5600	360 @ 4000	
	365 Horsepower..........V8-454	4 Barrel	4.251 x 4.00	454	8.50	365 @ 4800	465 @ 3200	
	425 Horsepower..........V8-454	4 Barrel	4.251 x 4.00	454	9.0	425 @ 5600	475 @ 4000	
1972	200 Horsepower②..........V8-350	4 Barrel	4.00 x 3.48	350	8.50	200 @ 4400	300 @ 2800	
	255 Horsepower②..........V8-350	4 Barrel	4.00 x 3.48	350	9.0	255 @ 5600	280 @ 4000	
	270 Horsepower②..........V8-454	4 Barrel	4.251 x 4.00	454	8.50	270 @ 4000	390 @ 3200	
1973	190 Horsepower②..........V8-350	4 Barrel	4.00 x 3.48	350	8.50	190 @ 4400	270 @ 2800	
	250 Horsepower②..........V8-350	4 Barrel	4.00 x 3.48	350	9.0	250 @ 5200	285 @ 4000	
	275 Horsepower②..........V8-454	4 Barrel	4.251 x 4.00	454	8.50	275 @ 4000	395 @ 2800	
1974	195 Horsepower②..........V8-350	4 Barrel	4.00 x 3.48	350	8.50	195 @ 4400	275 @ 2800	
	250 Horsepower②..........V8-350	4 Barrel	4.00 x 3.48	350	9.0	250 @ 5200	285 @ 4000	
	270 Horsepower②..........V8-454	4 Barrel	4.250 x 4.00	454	8.50	270 @ 4400	380 @ 2800	

①—Marketed as 396 cu. in. but actually 402 cu. in. ②—Ratings are net—As installed in the vehicle.

Year	Model	Cooling System Data			Thermostat Opening Temp.		Fuel Tank Gals.	Engine Oil			Transmissions			Rear Axle Pints
		Quarts No Heater	Quarts With Heater	Rad. Cap Relief Pressure				Refill Qts.③	Summer Grade	Winter Grade	Std. Pints	With Overdrive Pints	Automatic Qts. Refill	
1953–54	All	17¾	18¼	4	180	160	17¼	5	20W	10W	None	None	8	3½
1955	Six	17¾	18¼	4	180	160	17¼	5	20W	10W	None	None	5	4
	V8	16	17	7	180	160	17¼	5	20W	10W	None	None	5	4
1956	All	16	17	7	180	160	17¼	5	20W	10W	2	None	5	4
1957	All	16	17	7	180	160	16.4	5	20W	10W	2	None	5	4
1958	All	16	17	7	180	160	16.4	5	20W	10W	2	None	4½	4
1959	All	15½	16½	7	180	160	16.4	5	20W	10W	2	None	4½	4
1960	All	15½	16½	7	180	160	16.4	5	20W	10W	2	None	4½	4
1961–62	All	15½	16½	13	170	170	16.4	5	20W	10W	2	None	4½	4

continu

Year	Engine Model	Cooling System Data					Fuel Tank Gals.	Engine Oil			Transmissions		
		Quarts No Heater	Quarts With Heater	Rad. Cap Relief Pressure	Thermostat Opening Temp.			Refill Qts.	Summer Grade	Winter Grade	3 Speed Std. Pints	4 Speed Pints	Automatic Qts. Refill
963	250, 300 H.P.	15½	16½	13	180	...	20	4	20W	10W	2	...	
	340, 360 H.P.	15½	16½	13	180	...	20	5	20W	10W	2	...	
964	Std. Eng.	18	19	13	170	160	20	4	20W	10W	2	2½	
	Hi Perf.	18	19	13	170	160	20	5	20W	10W	2	2½	
965	250, 300 H.P.	18	19	13	180	...	20	4	20W	10W	2	2½	
	350, 365 H.P.	18	19	13	180	...	20	5	20W	10W	2	2½	
	375 H.P.	18	19	13	180	...	20	5	20W	10W	2	2½	

ar	Model or Engine	Cooling Capacity, Qts.			Radiator Cap Relief Pressure, Lbs.		Thermo. Opening Temp.	Fuel Tank Gals.	Engine Oil Refill Qts.	Transmission Oil		
		No Heater	With Heater	With A/C	With A/C	No A/C				3 Speed Pints	4 Speed Pints	Auto. Trans. Qts.
	8-327, 300 H.P.	15	16	16	15	15	180	20	4	2	2½	
	8-327, 350 H.P.	15	16	16	15	15	180	20	5	—	2½	—
	8-427, 425 H.P.	22	23	23	15	15	180	20	5	—	2½	—
	V8-327—300 H.P.	15	16	16	15	15	180	20	4	2	3	
	V8-327—350 H.P.	15	16	16	15	15	180	20	5	2	3	
	V8-427	22	23	23	15	15	180	20	5	2	3	
	8-327	14	15	15	15	15	195	20	4	3	3	
	8-427	21	22	22	15	15	195	20	5	3	3	
	8-350	14	15	15	15	15	195	20	4	3	3	
	8-427	21	22	22	15	15	195	20	5	3	3	
	8-350 Exc. 370 H.P.	14	15	21	15	15	195	20	4	—	3	
	8-350, 370 H.P.	17	18	22	15	15	180	20	4	—	3	
	8-454	21	22	—	15	15	195	20	5	—	3	
	8-350 Exc. 330 H.P.	14	15	15	15	15	195	18	4	—	3	—
	8-350 Exc. 330 H.P.	17	18	18	15	15	195	18	4	—	—	
	8-350, 330 H.P.	17	18	18	15	15	180	18	4	—	3	
	8-454, 365 H.P.	21	22	22	15	15	195	18	5	—	3	
	8-454, 425 H.P.	19	20	20	15	15	180	18	5	—	3	—
	8-454, 425 H.P.	21	22	22	15	15	180	18	5	—	—	
	8-350, 200 H.P.	16	17	18	15	15	195	18	4	—	3	4
	8-350, 255 H.P.	16	17	18	15	15	180	18	4	—	3	—
	8-454	22	23	24	15	15	195	18	5	—	3	4
	8-350, 190 H.P.	17	18	18	15	15	195	18	4	—	3	4
	8-350, 250 H.P.	17	18	18	15	15	180	18	4	—	3	4
	8-454, 275 H.P.	23	24	24	15	15	195	18	5	—	3	4
	8-350, 195 H.P.	—	—	—	15	15	195	18	4	—	3	—
	8-350, 250 H.P.	—	—	—	15	15	180	18	4	—	3	—
	8-454, 270 H.P.	—	—	—	15	15	195	18	4	—	3	—

Photos of damaged Corvettes courtesy of James H. Petrik

The Glass-Reinforced Plastic (GRP) body of the Corvette is distinctive for many reasons. Obviously, a major advantage of the material is the low cost to build. Another is the light weight, and still another is the ease with which it can be repaired. On the other side of the coin are its limitations, one of the chief of which is the damage that will result from fire.

Happily, most owners will never face this situation, but a glance at the photos on these pages should raise the serious question as to the wisdom of equipping your Corvette with a little-known factory option offered quietly since 1970, a portable light-weight fire extinguisher. With the damage that can result, it is surprising to note that of the 75 or so cars studied in the course of preparing material for this book, only one (right) was so equipped.

An excellent but little seen, accessory for *any* car is a fire extinguisher.

Some Notable Corvette Milestones

1953	Concept
1955	V-8 Engine 12 volt Electrical System
1956	3-Speed Manual Transmission Removable Hard Top Roll-Up Windows
1957	Ramjet Fuel Injection 4-Speed Manual Transmission
1958	Positraction Limited Slip Differential Dual Headlights
1962	327 CID V-8 Engine
1963	Sting Ray Sport Coupe Independent Rear Suspension Power Steering & Brakes Adjustable Steering Column Air Conditioning Rotating Headlights Aluminum Knock-Off Hub Wheels
1964	Quarter Panel Vents (Coupe only)
1965	Four Wheel Disc Brakes Optional Side Exhaust Pipes Turbo-Jet 396 V-8 Engine
1966	Turbo-Jet 427 V-8 Engine
1967	Rectangular Back Up Light Black Vinyl Covering for Hard Top
1968	Concealed Windshield Wipers Pop Up Headlights
1969	Anti-Theft Alarm System Tilt/Telescope Steering Wheel
1970	Turbo-Jet 454 V-8 Engine
1973	Concealed Bumpers

Quo Vadis, Corvette?

By 1975, the Corvette had evolved into a car that bore only vestigal signs of its heritage. Conceived as a "Sports" car, economic considerations of survival in a highly competitive market refined the car and caused the proliferation of characteristics more ideally suited to a "Luxury" car.

Heavy with air conditioning, tilting and telescoping steering wheel, super soft leather, AM/FM Stereo, plush carpeting, and with its mighty engine encumbered with federally-dictated smog-reducing filters, Corvette had become an entirely different car than was originally conceived. Undeniably different than the darting, youthful, Automotive Experience that was envisioned in 1953, it remains today to question its *future* directions.

One proposal, advanced by Gordon Buehrig, noted automobile Designer, would convert the Corvette chassis into a practical Grand Touring version. Other proposals have been made to add to the appearance of the Coupe by restyling its rear into the currently popular "fastback" style. Perhaps most likely is some form of a mid-engine Corvette resulting from Chevrolet's extensive work in that area.

Featuring a new rotary engine mounted transversely near the center of the car, an aerodynamic shape, and advanced instrumentation, the "mid-ship" engined Corvette has been a continuing consideration at Chevrolet.

Gordon M. Buehrig, retired automotive Designer, believes that a market exists for a Corvette designed, not for racing, but strictly for personal transportation. Based on a Corvette chassis, this preliminary design model incorporates an enormous trunk area and "Classic" car architecture.

What *ever* is done to the Corvette in its future, nothing can, however, change the characteristics of those that went before. With the growing popularity of automobile collecting as a hobby, scenes like that below are increasingly rare. Year by year, and with an increasing frequency, Corvette enthusiasts everywhere are withdrawing from the dismantling yards even *these* badly damaged cars for tender loving restoration. It's not yet too late for *you*!

Corvette Holding Area, T. Michaelis Corvettes, Napoleon, Ohio

Readers seeking additional information on Corvette are invited to consider:

CORVETTE NEWS
P.O. Box 7097, North End Station
Detroit, Michigan 48202

Published by the Chevrolet Division, CORVETTE NEWS is an excelle bi-monthly publication, professionally prepared, and containing much th is of interest to Corvette owners.

VETTE VUES MAGAZINE
P.O. Box 12182
Atlanta, Georgia 30305

Published every month, VETTE VUES contains technical tips, and news Corvette happenings. Its extensive advertising columns provide a most sigr ficant source for parts and services.

NATIONAL COUNCIL OF CORVETTE CLUBS
P. O. Box 325
Troy, Ohio 45373

A quasi-Official National organization of individuals and local Corvet Clubs, the NCCC publishes a fine bi-monthly magazine called BLUE BAR NCCC sanctions competition events and provides an orderly set of regul tions governing them.

VINTAGE CORVETTE CLUB OF AMERICA
2359 West Adams
Fresno, California 93706

Devoted to interest in the 1953-55 Corvettes, the VCCA presents in bi-monthly magazine, BLUE FLAME SPECIAL, items of historical sigr ficance, technical tips, and classified advertisements.

T. MICHAELIS CORVETTES
Route 1
Napoleon, Ohio 43545

Large parts Supplier. Offers excellent reference catalog which includes wid selection of both new and used parts. Free Brochure available on reques